WELCOME TO PRESIDENTS WHO BUILT AMERICA

Lunar Press is a privately-run publishing company that cares greatly about its content's accuracy.

If you notice any inaccuracies or have anything that you would like to discuss in the book, then please email us at lunarpresspublishers@gmail.com.

Enjoy!

CONTENTS

INTRODUCTION

There have been many great presidents of the United States, and there have been some we would rather forget. All of them made mistakes, and most did amazing things; that is what makes them human. Of course, there are those like George Washington and Abe Lincoln who will be forever remembered almost as superheroes—giants who represent everything that makes America great. These are the presidents who the rest have tried to live up to, but there have been some fantastic leaders who time seems to have left in the shadows.

In Greatest American Presidents for Kids, we will look at 20 of the most important presidents that have ruled the Land of the Free. Not all of them will be familiar, but most will. Some will surprise you, and you might even learn something new about the most famous ones on the list.

Remember that lists like this are subjective, so it is up to you, the reader, to decide who is your favorite. To make that easier, we have written about them in a less serious style so that you don't feel like you're in a boring classroom being spoken to by an even more boring teacher! We've added a Glossary at the end of the book where you can look up potentially unfamiliar words starred with asterisks.

In these pages, you will learn about modern presidents such as Barack Obama and Bill Clinton while also finding out about the lives of the Founding Fathers* such as

George Washington, Thomas Jefferson, and James Madison. We will also cover legends like John F. Kennedy, Dwight D. Eisenhower, and Franklin D. Roosevelt.

These were all extraordinary presidents, but there are some of the lesser-known guys, such as Woodrow Wilson and Grover Cleveland, who made massive improvements and changes throughout their time in office. All of these presidents were as important as the next and learning about them can be fun!

Learning doesn't have to be a chore, and when we find something that interests us, it can be a pleasure. We hope that this book sparks your interest and brings you a little closer to those that helped shape America.

Over two centuries have passed since George Washington was sworn in as the first president of the United States, and a lot has changed since then. But the fundamentals of what he and the other Founding Fathers laid down still remain. Have there been terrible things such as war and struggle in that period? Sure, but there has been a lot of good too.

History is about taking the rough with the smooth. Learning about the nasty moments in our past can be tough, but it is vitally important if we are to learn from our mistakes. If we as Americans—or just humans—don't understand our past, then how can we ever figure out where we want to end up?

This list has been organized in no particular order because it is up to us as individuals to decide the parts of history that we like and that we don't. Some presidents could just as easily have made it in and didn't. People like John Adams, Ulysses S. Grant, and James Garfield were great presidents, but they aren't covered here. It doesn't mean they weren't deserving of a spot. We just didn't choose them this time around!

So, turn to the next page and begin your journey along the presidential road. You might be shocked at times and inspired by others, but you will always learn something new, and that is the most amazing thing of all!

ABRAHAM LINCOLN

SERVED AS PRESIDENT	AGE AT INAUGURATION	PRESIDENT NUMBER
1861-1865	52	16TH
PARTY	**NICKNAME**	**HOMETOWN**
REPUBLICAN	HONEST ABE	LARUE COUNTY, KENTUCKY

BIOGRAPHY

Why not start off our list with one of the most famous American presidents of all time? Abraham Lincoln wasn't just a great leader; he was the man who ended slavery and steered his nation through the Civil War. He is the president who was immortalized forever when the Lincoln Memorial was built, and he continues to be a symbol for everything that is good about America.

Abraham Lincoln—or Abe, as he became known to most —was born on February 12, 1809, in a rural town in Kentucky. He was raised in a log cabin by his mother and father. They were considered poverty-stricken and uneducated, and this was something that always bothered young Abraham. At a time when public schools were rare, especially in the South, Abraham taught himself to read and write.

When his mother died, Abraham was only nine. It hit him hard, and he buried himself deeper in his education. For a period, he was raised by his 11-year-old sister. His father worked the land all day to make ends meet, and he had never been interested in the idea of studying and gaining an education. But these were all things that Abraham Lincoln knew people needed if they wanted to better themselves.

During these years, his father would claim that his son was lazy because he preferred learning over manual labor. It wasn't that Abe couldn't work in the fields—he was big and strong—he just knew that knowledge was the key. In fact, in his late teens and early twenties, Abe was known as one of the most dominant wrestlers in the South. He became county champion when he was 21, so he was very active!

As Abe became an adult, he moved to Illinois and taught himself law. America was booming at the time, and he knew that there was money to be made if a person had determination and education. He studied to be a lawyer and opened a bar with a friend. The partnership didn't last, as his business partner struggled with alcoholism, and Abe ended up doing all the work himself.

In the end, he sold his share in the bar and concentrated on practicing law. He passed his exams in 1837 and moved to a town called Springfield. There, he met his wife-to-be, Mary Todd, and they married soon after. They had four sons, but only one lived to adulthood. Abe was regarded as an extremely loving father.

After many years spent practicing law, Abe found himself being dragged toward politics. To those who knew him back then, he was charismatic and a strong public speaker. Whether he was sitting around a campfire or addressing a crowd in the town's square, people listened. With his big heart and bravery, it was like he was perfectly designed to be a great president.

Abe's first attempts at breaking into politics ended in defeat, but it only made him more determined. In 1858, he challenged Stephen A. Douglas for his place in the United States Senate*. Although he lost the vote, his popularity had only begun to grow. Abe knew this and figured that if he stuck at politics and gave it his all, he would succeed in the end.

This determination and popularity brought him to the

attention of the Republican Party, and he was asked to be their leader in their run for the U.S. presidency. In this race, he was again faced with Stephen A. Douglas as his opposition. This is important because Douglas believed democracy could work alongside slavery, while Abraham Lincoln was completely against slavery and oppression in all forms.

Unfortunately for Lincoln, the people of the southern states—where he was born and raised—were set on holding on to slavery. This meant he would always struggle to get them to vote for him, so Abe was fighting an uphill battle to be president from the beginning. Lincoln needed all of his charisma, passion, and public speaking ability to win the majority vote.

His determination paid off, and on March 4, 1861, Abraham Lincoln was sworn in as the 16th president of the United States. His appointment sparked huge anger from the South, and they rose up against him. Eleven of the southern states separated themselves from the rest, becoming the Confederates. The northern states remained in the Union.

The South wanted slavery to continue, as the free labor increased their profits drastically. Lincoln had always believed that every human being was born equal, so he opposed slavery. When the Confederates fired on Fort Sumter on April 12, 1861, the American Civil War began.

The war raged for four years and threatened to rip the country apart. Still, Abe stood firm on his beliefs, and on January 1, 1863, he issued the Emancipation Proclamation. This was a new national law declaring that slavery was to be forever abolished. In doing this, Abe is reported to have instantly freed 3.5 million African

Americans from slavery. Although there was still a massively long road ahead in giving African Americans complete freedom, it was the single biggest event in the history of liberty.

With the war still in full flow, his Emancipation Proclamation didn't go down well in the ten states that remained loyal to the Confederates. But some of them were starting to see sense and would gradually swear their allegiance to the Union. In one of the most memorable moments of the Civil War, Lincoln gave a speech at Gettysburg on November 19, 1863. In what became known as the Gettysburg Address, he asked for freedom and liberty among all of the American people.

The war ended on May 26, 1865, but a lot of damage had been done. Although the whole country was united under a single American flag once more, a rift between the northern and southern states had been made so deep that some of the aftereffects would remain to this day. Still, Abe won his reelection in 1865 with a landslide vote, and he had truly become a darling of the people.

But so many of those that had been loyal to the Confederates had remained that way despite the war ending. One of those men was John Wilkes Booth, a stage actor and Confederate spy from Maryland.

On April 14, 1865, only a month after being reelected, Abe Lincoln and his wife attended a play at Ford's Theatre in Washington, D.C. As Abe watched from one of the boxes, John Wilkes Booth crept up behind and shot the president in the back of the head. After the assassin had fled, Abe was taken to a hospital close by, where he fell into a coma. The wounds were too much, even for someone as strong as Abraham Lincoln, and he died eight hours later.

His killer was tracked down and killed by police two weeks later, but the loss of the 16th president would last forever. He was a man who believed in freedom and loving one's country. He was someone that changed the way America viewed civil rights forever, and he did everything he could in his life to help those less fortunate.

On May 30, 1922, 57 years after Abe died, his memory was solidified forever with the completion of the Lincoln Memorial in Washington, D.C. It took eight years to build, but it will always stand tall as a reminder to everyone that true greatness only comes from doing good.

FRANKLIN D. ROOSEVELT

SERVED AS PRESIDENT	AGE AT INAUGURATION	PRESIDENT NUMBER
1933-1945	51	32ND
PARTY	**NICKNAME**	**HOMETOWN**
DEMOCRATS	FDR	HYDE PARK, NEW YORK

BIOGRAPHY

The man who would become lovingly known as FDR will be forever remembered as a great president and as the only one to have served four terms in office. His 13 years as president saw him oversee many major events, including World War II and the Great Depression* (1929–1940). During his time in the White House, he became one of the most well-respected American presidents of all time.

Franklin D. Roosevelt was born on January 30, 1882, in Hyde Park, New York, to wealthy and influential parents. He was a distant cousin of Teddy Roosevelt, who was the president himself for two terms between 1901 and 1909. Even though FDR came from a family with plenty of money, he grew up to be considered a man of the everyday people.

As a child, he loved to sail, hunt, and play piano. He was also very good at sports, especially golf and tennis. At a time when vacations for most American families involved perhaps traveling to the next state at most, the Roosevelts regularly visited Europe. By the time Franklin was 15, he had been to most European countries and had become fluent in German and French.

In 1900, at the age of 18, FDR got into Harvard. There, he met his soon-to-be wife, Eleanor, and they had five children together. Although he did well at Harvard, he found himself getting drawn toward law. Four years later, he moved on to Columbia University, where he left with a law degree and a promising career ahead of him.

Much like his time at Harvard, FDR soon became bored with being a lawyer. Well, maybe not bored, but he had found something that excited him more than anything else—politics.

His rise up the political ladder was rapid. By 1910, he had already become a senator for the state of New York. His no-nonsense approach to his work caught the attention of then-president Woodrow Wilson (we'll cover him later!). Soon Franklin was asked to become secretary of the U.S. Navy. Like everything FDR tried, he did this perfectly and thoroughly. He remained in this high position for seven years before he decided that it was time for more.

In 1920, when Franklin was only 38, he ran for the vice presidency. He didn't win the election—in fact, he lost by a landslide—but he showed massive promise in his ability to campaign. In politics, campaigning is one of the most important aspects as it lets the people see the person they will be voting for in all of their glory. Of course, it can backfire when that person isn't good at it, but FDR was a man of the people, and it shone through in his speeches.

A year after his unsuccessful attempt to become vice president, FDR lost the use of his legs when he was paralyzed after contracting polio* during a trip to Maine. This might have slowed him down in his pursuit to reach the White House, but instead, it spurred him on. He continued to campaign, but this time he took a different route.

Knowing that he had probably tried for too much too early in 1920, FDR ran for the position of governor of New York and won. While in power, he clamped down heavily on the corruption* and greed that had infested the system. His work at cleaning out the bad guys from office made the public love him even more, as they now knew that he was completely on their side.

When the Wall Street Crash* in 1929 threatened to bring America to its knees, the voters knew they needed someone strict and determined in power. When the next election rolled around, they voted for FDR in the hopes that he could reproduce what he did in New York for the whole nation.

During his inauguration, Franklin told the people that they had "nothing to fear but fear itself," rallying everyone who had lost their jobs and giving them all hope. Within his first 100 days in office, Roosevelt tightened budgets and lowered wages for government officials. With the money saved, he filtered it down to the less wealthy workers on the streets. His strategy to gradually bring America back to economic stability was called the New Deal.

Due to his positive changes, America started to get back on its feet over time. When the next election rolled around in 1932, FDR won easily. The margin between votes for him and his losing competitor, Herbert Hoover (we won't cover him later!), was the largest in over 100 years. Franklin Roosevelt was now truly one of the most trusted and adored presidents in American history.

In 1939, the rumblings of World War II began in Europe, but FDR was adamant the Americans wouldn't get involved. They had their own issues to deal with on home soil, with the Great Depression still several years away from ending. He concentrated all of his efforts on getting America out of the economic disaster that had befallen them, and he was eventually successful.

Unfortunately, the joy of America finally coming out of the Great Depression in 1940 didn't last very long. On December 7, 1941, the Japanese bombed Pearl Harbor, and America declared war. Four days later, Germany declared war on the US, and FDR and his people were officially dragged into World War II.

By 1944, Roosevelt had already been in office for twelve years and three terms, so it was thought that he wouldn't run for a fourth term. Still, he hadn't been expected to go for it the third time either, but he had and won. This was partly to do with the war being in full flow, and this same reason helped him remain as president when he won election number four in November of 1944.

Most of the public was unaware of just how bad FDR's health was at the time, though, and he only stayed in office for a year of his fourth term. He died on April 12, 1945, while still the president. But the worst war in history was about to end, and he had saved the nation from the worst recession in its history.

At his funeral, as his coffin was being loaded into the presidential train, it is said that a penniless man in the crowd began crying hysterically. When someone asked if he knew Franklin Roosevelt personally, he is said to have replied, "No, but he knew me."

Although this story might just be a tale, it still sums up the 32nd president perfectly. He was a man of the people and genuinely cared about everyone.

GEORGE WASHINGTON

SERVED AS PRESIDENT	AGE AT INAUGURATION	PRESIDENT NUMBER
1789-1797	57	1ST
PARTY	**NICKNAME**	**HOMETOWN**
No Party	Father of His Country	Westmoreland County, Virginia

BIOGRAPHY

What sets George Washington apart from all other American presidents is that before he was given that honor, the position didn't even exist. American freedom, liberty, and the pursuit of happiness all began with one man. He will forever be remembered as the Father of the United States and someone who believed in everything that is still good about the country, but his path to greatness was bumpy and hard.

George Washington was born on February 22, 1732, in Westmoreland County, Virginia. At the time, America was ruled by the British crown, but some states had grown weary of the high taxes and not having their own nationality. Washington felt strongly about this, but he'd always dreamed of joining the military, which just so happened to be run by the British.

Despite this desire, he continued to study hard. He knew that fighting would only get his people so far. To really make a difference, he would need a good education to back it up. As a child, he excelled in trigonometry, mathematics, and map-making. By all reports, he was an energetic boy who always tried to do right.

His hopes of joining the military were realized in 1753, and at the age of 20, George was sent to the front line to fight in the French and Indian War. Two years later, Washington and his platoon were ambushed during the Battle of Monongahela. Although they suffered casualties, his bravery and courage were recognized, and he was promoted to chief of all Virginia forces.

Ironically, the British forces he was fighting alongside would become his enemies in the end, but that is all much later in his story.

When Washington returned from his military service, he fell in love with Martha Custis. Martha had been recently widowed, and her late husband had left behind a sprawling plantation. Washington took control of the land and its many tobacco and wheat fields. He set about making the place as efficient as possible, and in a few years, the Washington family was one of the wealthiest in Virginia.

During this time, Washington made small strides into politics, running for local office and representing Frederick County in the House of Burgesses* for seven years. By the 1760s, he had gained the trust of landowners and the common people alike. Most people shared his view on British taxation and how unfair it was to the US.

On June 14, 1775, Washington was made commander-in-chief of the Continental Army, a group of landowners and soldiers who would oppose British rule once and for all. Washington had been turned down for promotion by the British Army years before, and he always held a grudge about that. He was determined to free America from Britain, and to do that, they needed to go to war.

With this decision, the world saw the beginning of the American Revolutionary War.

Once he had charge of the Continental Army*, Washington stormed Boston in March 1776, defeating the British and forcing them back. The British evacuated Boston, and Washington moved his forces into New

York. His victory didn't last, and a few months later, they were forced to flee. This began a string of defeats for Washington and his Patriots, but he never lost faith.

His ability to rally his troops and fight again worried the British. The revolution that was taking place on American soil wouldn't fade away as others had before, and the British knew they were facing a great man.

On July 4, 1776, one of the most important days in American history occurred while George Washington was on the front line with the creation of the Declaration of Independence. It was originally written by Thomas Jefferson and then edited by John Adams and Benjamin Franklin. The Declaration of Independence basically declared the 13 North American colonies would no longer accept British rule.

Washington used guerilla tactics* and continued to attack British camps, often under cover of night. Over Christmas, he won major battles in Princeton and Trenton, but his Continental Army ended up snowed-in at Valley Forge. This long, harsh winter nearly broke their resistance. Most of the men were barefoot, and the Patriots lost many limbs to frostbite. Several people died due to the conditions.

Throughout the stages of the war that followed, Washington continued to encourage his troops. In October 1781, the Patriots won the last major battle of the Revolutionary War when the British fleet surrendered at Yorktown.

Two years later, in 1783, Washington returned home to his family. The war had officially ended on September 3, 1783, and the man who had led his forces against the mighty British and won felt like he had done more than enough. But his retirement wouldn't last, and defeating the British had only been the beginning of the tale for a new nation.

In September of 1787, the Constitution was drawn up for the first time. It would go through many stages and disagreements over the next couple of years. In the end, George Washington was sworn in as the first president of the United States in New York City on April 30, 1789. It was a day that will always remain vitally important in the history of America.

Following his appointment as president, George Washington began discussing a declaration that would explain the rights his new American people had in their pursuit of happiness and freedom. This would become known as the Bill of Rights. Now, the citizens of America knew that they could challenge the government when laws or taxes seemed unfair, and they could then put it to the vote. It gave the people of America the right to pursue whatever religion they chose and that freedom of speech would be respected. This is the basis of democracy.

George Washington led the new, independent nation from his offices in New York, and he did so for two terms. He was loved by the people because he made changes that helped them. Like all good leaders, he understood those he ruled over. He made many changes, mainly regarding freedom and liberty, and these have become the cornerstone of the United States ever since.

One of his big beliefs was that a country should only be ruled by one person or party for a certain period of time. Once that was over, the people would vote for the next president. He had seen what happened to nations run by kings and queens. He believed that since they could never be challenged, they could raise taxes, change laws, and do whatever they liked forever. This sort of rule is the exact opposite of democracy.

In March of 1797, George Washington finished his second term as president and retired, just as he promised he would. He returned to his plantation in Mount Vernon and lived out the last two years of his life simply as a proud American. He died on December 14, 1799, after his health had declined rapidly. The exact cause will never be known, but one of the doctors called to his home put it down to an inflamed throat.

He left behind a new America—one that believes in the freedom of expression and liberty. George Washington is thought of by some as the greatest American president that ever lived, but either way, he will forever be the first. In that sense, he had it harder than all that came after him, so he can certainly be seen as America's greatest revolutionary.

THOMAS JEFFERSON

SERVED AS PRESIDENT	AGE AT INAUGURATION	PRESIDENT NUMBER
1801-1809	57	3RD

PARTY	NICKNAME	HOMETOWN
DEMOCRATIC-REPUBLICAN	FATHER OF THE DECLARATION OF INDEPENDENCE	CHARLOTTESVILLE, VIRGINIA

BIOGRAPHY

The man who wrote the Declaration of Independence for the previous president on our list was Thomas Jefferson. It is considered the most important document in American history, and it stands for everything that George Washington, Thomas Jefferson, and the other Founding Fathers dreamed of for their country.

Born in Shadwell, Virginia, on April 13, 1743, Thomas Jefferson was raised on his father's prosperous plantation. His family's wealth meant that he had a fantastic education—something that was only reserved for a small few in the 18th century—and he took full advantage of that.

He was a voracious reader, finishing his father's entire 20-book library by the time he was six. His tutors were flabbergasted by his progress, and by nine, the young Thomas was fluent in Latin, French, and Greek. But his education stalled momentarily when his father died in 1757, leaving the 14-year-old with his family's estate, including livestock, property, and crops.

As he reached his 18th birthday, Thomas decided that tending to his prosperous land could wait. He left it in the care of trusted family members and set off for the College of William & Mary. Once there, he fell in love with both science and politics, but he knew that wouldn't be enough if he were to become an influential politician.

Like most of the presidents on this list, Jefferson moved on to studying law. After he had passed the bar*, he practiced law for eight years between 1767 and 1775. This was followed pretty quickly by his first real venture into politics when he was elected to serve in Virginia's House of Burgesses. But just as he was finding his feet in office, tensions with the British had begun to get heated.

The American Revolutionary War was about to break out, and Thomas Jefferson would play a massive role in it all.

Jefferson was asked to write the first draft of the Declaration of Independence in 1776. It would be the first time in modern history that a nation declared itself independent from a ruling power such as the British. The Declaration of Independence that he created would become the template for many countries over the next 200 years in their efforts to break free from oppression. He was only 33 when he wrote it.

As the war raged and George Washington and his army fought the British in Boston and other states, Thomas Jefferson returned home to Virginia. He was quickly elected as governor of the House of Burgesses and set to making a positive difference. While in power, he changed many laws, including the Virginia Statute for Religious Freedom, which ended up being the First Amendment on the Bill of Rights years later.

In 1789, George Washington made Jefferson his Secretary of State after seeing what a fantastic leader and thinker he was. This didn't go too well for Jefferson, though. He ended up having many conflicts with others in office, mainly due to disagreements about rights and certain laws. In fact, he resigned in 1793, feeling that he would need to be president himself if he was to make a real difference.

His chance came in the elections of 1796 after George Washington retired. Another of the Founding Fathers, John Adams, defeated Jefferson, making Adams the second president of the United States. The loss wasn't all bad, as Thomas Jefferson was named vice president, a role he carried out brilliantly until the next election in 1800.

The first of these elections is so important because both sides of the vote were heavily split in opinion. One side wanted Thomas Jefferson to be named the next president, while the other voted for his opponent, Aaron Burr. The voting was heated, and there were rumors of another civil war breaking out.

But when they became independent, America had decided to be a democratic nation, and if democracy is to work, then every person's vote must count equally. This also means that the losing side needs to accept that the majority of citizens chose the winner, and they should live in peace with the final result.

For the first time in Western* history, a peaceful changing of power took place when both parties that were challenging each other held completely opposing views. It was the American experiment and passed its first real test with flying colors.

Thomas Jefferson was sworn in as the 3rd president of the United States on March 4, 1801. It was the first time this had been done in the new capital, Washington D.C., and it marked the beginning of a wonderful period in American history.

In his time in office, Thomas Jefferson cut the national debt in half and then doubled the size of the United

States with the Louisiana Purchase (discussed later in the book) in 1903. He ordered the expedition of Lewis and Clark, who explored and mapped the vast new land that America had just bought. It is generally considered the most famous and loved expedition of all time, with many books and movies being made about it since.

After two terms as president, Thomas Jefferson retired to his home in Virginia. He didn't put his feet up for long and founded the University of Virginia, going so far as to design its campus himself. He was named the first president of the college and continued to promote education as the greatest of all rights given to us as human beings.

Amazingly, on July 4, 1826, Thomas Jefferson died on the day of the 50th anniversary of the Declaration of Independence—the same one that he wrote and helped create. The declaration states that all people should have freedom and liberty and a chance to make their own life.

He left behind an America that was still only getting used to its independence, but he did so with a nation twice the size and wealthier. America was on the verge of becoming the most influential and powerful country in the world, and it was all thanks to visionaries and leaders such as Thomas Jefferson.

ANDREW JACKSON

SERVED AS PRESIDENT	AGE AT INAUGURATION	PRESIDENT NUMBER
1829-1837	61	7TH

PARTY	NICKNAME	HOMETOWN
DEMOCRATS	OLD HICKORY	LANCASTER, SOUTH CAROLINA

BIOGRAPHY

Andrew Jackson was an army general who won major battles against the British. He was a man who came from poverty and educated himself to become the 7th president of the United States. And it is his face we still see on $20 bills.

Surprisingly, Andrew Jackson is sometimes forgotten in lists of great American presidents, despite being one of the main reasons democracy is still here today. But there were things about Andrew Jackson's time in office that were not so nice, and we need to remember them too.

Born in Carolina on March 15, 1767, Andrew Jackson never knew his father, who was also named Andrew. Andrew Senior was a logger who had emigrated to America from Ulster, Ireland, in 1765. In a time when there were no safety regulations and workers were forced to do their jobs under great danger, his father died while cutting down trees three months before Andrew was born.

Without his father's income, the family struggled to put food on the table. This meant that education wasn't an option for Andrew and his two older brothers. Soon after his father's death, the Jacksons moved in with their aunt and uncle in Lancaster, South Carolina. Andrew claims this as his true birthplace and his home.

Andrew's mother dreamed of him becoming a minister, and her need to push him in this direction gave her son the chance he needed to get his education. At the time, schooling for potential ministers was free, and Andrew learned how to read and write through his religious teachings. He also excelled in mathematics, Greek, and Latin, among other things.

When he was ten years old, the American Revolutionary War broke out, and the young boy felt his passion for his nation's freedom rising even at that young age. In fact, he signed up for the American militia* three years later. Amazingly, he was accepted despite him only being 13. He worked as a courier, running from one platoon to the other, delivering messages.

During the war, he received the devastating news that his mother had died. This made him an orphan at 14, but it also stirred up a hatred for British rule that was to stay with him for the rest of his life.

By the time he was old enough for college, he was seen as too poverty-stricken for such an elite education. Andrew didn't let that stop him, and he studied (you guessed it... law!) by himself. He read every book he could find on the subject and managed to pass the bar in 1787. He was soon working as a successful prosecuting attorney* in North Carolina. The boy who couldn't afford an education had earned one of the country's most esteemed careers through his determination!

Andrew practiced law for many years but was called back into military action again—this time as an adult—when war broke out in 1812. By 1814, he was made a general and led his men to victory in the Battle of Horseshoe Bend. His most famous and important military triumph came a year later when he defeated the British at the Battle of New Orleans.

Although the victory made him a national hero, many of the tactics and slaughtering of people have led some historians to paint him as a nasty leader. War is always violent and nasty, though. Andrew Jackson was no different from thousands of generals in the past who led their armies into battle and caused bloodshed.

After the war ended, the Americans cut funding for the military, and Jackson returned home. As part of his compensation for his fantastic service to the army, he was made governor of Florida. This was his first solid entry into politics, and even though he didn't have much previous experience, he was determined to succeed.

His role as a leader in the army served him well, and his reputation as a war hero and a man of the people made him very popular. So much so that he was soon being tipped as a presidential candidate for the 1824 elections. Jackson's dreams of becoming the 6th president of the United States didn't come true, though.

In that particular election, he was up against John Quincy Adams, who is not to be confused with John Adams, the 2nd president. Confusing, I know! Now, when Jackson ran for the presidency in 1824, John Quincy Adams was expected by most to win. This proved to be true, and Andrew Jackson was forced to wait a little while longer before he could walk into the White House and take his place in history.

Instead of being deterred, Jackson decided to campaign for the next election the day after his defeat. In the years between 1824 and 1828, Jackson and his party decided to start a smear campaign* against President Adams. They pointed out his snobbishness to the public and claimed he didn't care about the lower classes. It worked, and

John Q. Adams only lasted one term.

Andrew Jackson went on to win the 1828 election, becoming the 7th president of the United States. He instantly set about trying to clear the national debt and showing the nation that he was just as hard-working as they were. He claimed that the voice of the people needed to be heard, and they loved him for it because he listened when they spoke.

He was sworn in on March 4, 1829, and quickly began replacing many of the cabinet* members. Jackson believed that John Q. Adams's cabinet had been crooked, and his investigations found that millions of dollars (in today's money) had been stolen. His discovery made the public trust him even more, as they saw that he was going to run things fairly.

As is mentioned at the beginning of this chapter, Andrew Jackson had a dark side. His belief that Native Indians needed to be run out of the country was disgusting and inexcusable. He also believed in slavery, as did many white Americans back then. These widespread views made it a very shameful time in American history and something that can never be ignored.

Thankfully we don't see things that way anymore, and we must never forget that we are all equal in every way.

Jackson was reelected without much threat of losing in 1832. In what was probably his crowning achievement as president, he cleared the national debt for the first and only time in American history.

Another record that belongs to him is that he was the first American president to have an assassination attempt on his life. As he was leaving the Capitol Building one evening in January 1835, a man pulled a pistol on him. It misfired, and Jackson managed to restrain the assassin with his cane until help arrived.

He stepped down from his role as president after two terms in office and moved back home to see out the rest of his days in peace. Andrew Jackson died of heart failure at the grand old age of 78. He passed away on his deathbed with all of his family around him, where he supposedly told his children not to cry, as he would see them someday on the other side.

Andrew Jackson left behind a presidential legacy that still splits opinions to this day. It is up to us as individuals to decide which view we take on it. Freedom to choose is one of the main aspects of democracy, after all!

THEODORE ROOSEVELT

SERVED AS PRESIDENT	AGE AT INAUGURATION	PRESIDENT NUMBER
1901-1909	42	26TH
PARTY	**NICKNAME**	**HOMETOWN**
REPUBLICAN	TEDDY	NEW YORK CITY

BIOGRAPHY

Affectionately known as Teddy, Theodore Roosevelt remains the youngest person to become president in the history of America. In his lifetime, he strived to help the average worker and tried to get fair pay for all. He was a lover of nature and raised millions to help build national parks and forests all over the country. Also, he was a distant cousin of the 32nd president, Franklin Roosevelt!

Theodore Roosevelt Jr. was born on October 27, 1858, in Manhattan, New York. His family was wealthy, and he grew up with the best education available to him. Although he was sickly as a child—he had asthma, among other things—little Teddy was still an energetic child. He was curious and passionate, two traits that helped him become what some historians claim to be the first modern president.

When Teddy was only six, he witnessed the funeral of Abraham Lincoln, and the experience stayed with him his whole life. As the casket was led through the streets of New York City, he watched it from the second-floor window of his grandfather's mansion. Seeing everyone paying their respects to the great Abe Lincoln inspired his passion for becoming a leader someday.

Due to his poor health, he spent his early years being homeschooled by his parents and tutors, but it was still an excellent education. Even though Teddy grew up with asthma, he fought it by training and exercising as much as possible. He refused to let it hold him back, which is a great view to have on life and something that can inspire everyone!

When he became a young adult, he decided to attend Harvard University in 1876 and graduated after four years with near-perfect grades. I think we can all guess what he studied in college, and if you said "law," then give yourself a gold star! His love for law faded somewhat in the years following his graduation, though, and soon Teddy was looking for a new challenge.

After considering many other ways to find his path, Teddy settled on politics. He was an excellent speaker, knew the law, and had wealth, so it seemed like the perfect fit. Also, his ancestors and distant cousins, such as Franklin Roosevelt, all had a history in politics. This made it easier for him to edge his way in the door, which meant that he was already one step ahead.

Teddy started his road to the White House by first earning his position as the police commissioner of New York City in 1895. His strict approach to how he ran the police caught the attention of then-president William McKinley, and in 1897, he was named as U.S. Navy assistant secretary. It was a great honor and one in which Teddy took a lot of pride. It would never be enough, though, and he soon had his sights set on an even higher position.

His next step up the political ladder came when he was given the important role of governor of New York. When the Spanish-American War broke out in April 1898, Roosevelt resigned from his post with the U.S. Navy and formed the First U.S. Volunteer Cavalry regiment. Their aim was to advance on Cuba and end the conflict before it really had a chance to get going, but he needed to get men to sign up and fight for nothing more than their pride. The newspapers fell in love with his rag-tag group and named them the "Rough Riders."

Teddy trained this makeshift army himself, which included professional athletes, cowboys, Native Americans, miners, hunters, and sheriffs. They were seen as modern-day celebrities, the type of characters people read about in old action novels about the Wild West! To the public, Teddy and his men were a brave group of heroes that were willing to die for their country's freedom.

When the Rough Riders marched to Kettle Hill, Cuba, in July 1898 and forced their Spanish opponents to surrender, Teddy Roosevelt returned to America as a national hero. He was viewed as a true American, and with his Ivy League* education, his next step up in politics seemed like it was only a matter of time.

In fact, it happened so fast that even Teddy himself must have been pleasantly surprised!

Two years after the Rough Riders had won their battles in Cuba, Teddy was named vice president of the United States. He was to serve under the man who had also promoted him to the assistant secretary of the U.S. Navy, William McKinley. Most people knew that Teddy would one day be named president, so his role as vice president seemed natural.

He wouldn't need an election to give him his first term in office. In the end, it was a national tragedy that meant he got there without the voters' help.

A year after Teddy had become vice president, William McKinley was assassinated on September 14, 1901. It meant that America needed to elect someone else, and Theodore Roosevelt was quickly sworn in as the 26th president of the United States. It wouldn't have been how Teddy wanted to do it, but he found himself in the White House, nonetheless.

Already loved by the public, few people argued about the promotion of their new president, and his time in charge was heavily influenced by his calmness under pressure. He managed to end the Coal Strike of 1902 before it really began, getting better pay for the workers and settling any further disputes. Teddy also brought in strict laws regarding food and medicine, meaning that regular checks had to be done to make sure what was being sold to the public was of the highest quality.

One of President Roosevelt's biggest achievements and something which showed his ability to settle disputes without violence was when he played a significant role in ending the Russo-Japanese War* (1904–1905). His actions earned him a Nobel Peace Prize the following year, which only goes to show how much of a difference one person can make when they are determined and kind-hearted.

There was one achievement Teddy was most proud of— his work in preserving national resources, new laws protecting wildlife, and more funding for national parks. His work in these areas was met with stern opposition from logging companies, hunters, and many others. But Teddy never backed down, and the changes he made for the good of nature helped save many species and forests from being destroyed.

Teddy Roosevelt served two very successful terms as president and could have easily won a third if he had run. He loved his job, but he had promised in 1904 that he would bow out of the elections when his second term ended. He kept his word, as he always believed that two terms were just enough time before a presidency became a dictatorship*.

William Howard Taft succeeded him in 1909, but Teddy was still a young man as far as retiring presidents go. He stayed involved in politics, appearing at many campaign rallies and giving speeches at colleges. During one of these events in Milwaukee, Wisconsin, Teddy was shot at by a man named John Schrank.

Schrank was a barkeeper who claimed that former president William McKinley's ghost had ordered him to kill Theodore Roosevelt! If Schrank's bullet hadn't been slowed down by a speech Teddy had in his jacket pocket before it stuck in his chest, the 26th president of the United States might have died.

Thankfully, he survived for another seven years and would be forever loved by the American people. He died in his sleep at the age of 60, leaving behind a legacy that not many other presidents have, would, or will ever match.

HARRY S. TRUMAN

SERVED AS PRESIDENT	AGE AT INAUGURATION	PRESIDENT NUMBER
1945-1953	60	33RD
PARTY	**NICKNAME**	**HOMETOWN**
DEMOCRATS	GIVE 'EM HELL HARRY	INDEPENDENCE, MISSOURI

BIOGRAPHY

One interesting thing about Harry S. Truman is that the "S" in his name doesn't actually stand for anything! He was given the letter "S" as a middle name in honor of his two grandfathers, Solomon Young and Anderson Shipp Truman. Apparently, this was quite a common practice at the time.

Apart from this fun fact about his middle name, Truman was also the person who made the final and devastating decision to drop an atomic bomb on Japan. Of course, there is much more to his time as president than this single moment, and that is what we are going to learn about.

Born into a farming family in Independence, Missouri, on May 8, 1884, Harry Truman did not have access to the sort of college education a lot of the presidents on this list had. In fact, he is the only American president in the 20th century without one. He was very intelligent; he just didn't have the degrees or paperwork to back it up.

He never let his family's lack of wealth hold him back, though. He loved to study history, read books, and practice music. His mother was very encouraging and showed him full support in whatever path he chose. This was important, as the rest of his family had expected Harry to stay working on the family's farm like his father had, not chase his political dreams in Washington.

But by the time he was a teenager, Harry had started to edge away from farming life, and he got a job as a clerk in a local mailroom. He respected his father—and all those who worked hard at whatever they did—but he dreamed of making a big difference. He always stayed true to his humble upbringing and respect for the average worker, which brought him closer to the hearts of the people years later when he ran for president.

When his family began to struggle with the farm in 1906, he returned to his home to work the land and help out. He did this for another 11 years until America entered World War I (1914–1918), and his patriotism meant that he was always going to fight. Truman joined the American Army in 1917 when he was 33, which was pretty old for such a dangerous job. He didn't care, and he quickly climbed to the rank of captain.

Truman was shipped off to France to the horrific battles taking place there. He was named as a battery commander, and in all his time on the front line, he never lost a single soldier under his command. He was seen as a brave leader but also calm and smart under pressure.

He returned to Missouri as a hero and decided to settle down with his new wife, Bess, and opened a small men's clothing store. Harry Truman—like all presidents—was someone who needed to keep challenging himself. This was something that would eventually lead him to the White House, but he had a long way to go before then!

His journey into politics began in 1922 when he was elected to be a judge in his county court. By all accounts, Truman loved this role. He may not have studied law at Harvard or some Ivy League college like many others on our list, but he still managed to be a big success.

Truman continued in this role for many years, and it wasn't until 1934 that he really made his mark in politics. He ran for and won an election to the U.S. Senate and spent his first term learning his trade and finding his way. Truman kept his head down, but he saw many things about how the government was being run that he didn't like—mainly the corruption.

Truman was disgusted by the Senate's lavish spending and the money they wasted on themselves. By his second term, he was confident enough to take these cheaters on. He set up what is now known as The Truman Committee, whose job was to catch those who were stealing taxpayers' money.

It worked, and it is said that Truman and his committee saved the country $15 million. In today's money, that number is, wait for it... $220 billion! That is quite a saving, wouldn't you agree?

After that, things changed pretty drastically for Truman. The public loved him, and they hated the idea of the taxes they paid being stolen by the people they had trusted with it. News had gotten out about the huge amount of money the government had been wasting, and they weren't happy. They wanted honest and hard-working leaders, and Harry S. Truman fit that role perfectly.

In 1944, Truman was encouraged to run for the vice presidency and easily won the election. He was now second in command to the great Franklin D. Roosevelt, a man we've already learned was a hater of corruption too. They were a perfect fit and just what the American people needed to bring them through the end of World War II (1939–1945).

As we know, Franklin D. Roosevelt had just begun his record-breaking fourth term in office when Truman became his vice president. When FDR's bad health failed him 82 days after Truman's appointment, the farmer's kid from Missouri was sworn in as president on April 12, 1945.

One of his first decisions as American president will be forever seen as a dark day in human history, but it also went some way in ending the war. On April 6 and 9, 1945, the Americans dropped two atomic bombs on Hiroshima and Nagasaki. It was the first time in history that an atomic bomb had been used in this way, and the terrible explosions killed nearly 250,000 people.

War, as we've discussed, is a horrible, ugly thing. Unfortunately, it is still part of who we are as human beings. For those who have to make the decisions as Harry S. Truman did, the guilt must stay with them until the day they die. But who knows how long the war might have continued if he hadn't done it? Would more innocent people have died over time? These are the questions that can never have any real answers, unfortunately.

Truman saw much pain and suffering in his time as president, but he handled most of it well. Europe had been devastated by World War II, and he spent millions helping to rebuild the countries ruined by German bombs. He formed alliances with European nations that still last to this day, and America became the superpower we know today.

But wars were still breaking out across the globe, despite the devastation of World War II. America was soon dragged into the Korean War, which the public didn't like. The Cold War with Russia had also begun, so Truman struggled to keep the American people on his side. Like the rest of the planet, they were sick and saddened by the endless death and destruction.

Truman stayed in the presidency until January 1953, when he left office without running for a third term. The American war hero Dwight Eisenhower (we'll cover him soon!) was going to be his opponent in the upcoming election, and Truman probably knew he didn't have a chance of winning against him.

Harry S. Truman retired to his home in Independence, Missouri, and lived out the rest of his life in peace. He stayed away from politics and the newspapers and died the day after Christmas on December 26, 1972, at the age of 88. He was given a quiet, inexpensive funeral, which had been his last wish, and left the world as the American president who helped end the evilest war in human history.

WOODROW WILSON

SERVED AS PRESIDENT	AGE AT INAUGURATION	PRESIDENT NUMBER
1913-1921	56	28TH

PARTY	NICKNAME	HOMETOWN
DEMOCRATS	THE PROFESSOR	STAUNTON, VIRGINIA

BIOGRAPHY

For some reason, Woodrow Wilson is one of the lesser-known American presidents. This is strange because he achieved so much, including bringing an end to World War I. He globalized democracy and helped promote women's rights. He might not be thought of as fondly as some of the others on this list, but he was a humble soul and probably would have wanted it that way!

Thomas Woodrow Wilson was born in Staunton, Virginia, on December 28, 1856. His father, Joseph Ruggles Wilson, was a well-respected pastor, and Woodrow was raised in a very religious household. His mother and father were also very set in the ways of the Confederate States of America, which was a strong opinion to take at a time when the Civil War was just beginning to rumble.

Despite his parents being Confederates, his grandfather —who had emigrated to the States from Ireland—was actually the publisher of an anti-slavery newspaper. This meant that Woodrow was brought up seeing both sides of American beliefs. His family wasn't wealthy, and young Woodrow struggled with dyslexia his whole life. He refused to let it disrupt his studies, and he excelled in philosophy and history in high school.

Another of his passions while at school was the debate team. Woodrow was a fine public speaker, and he had a way of being able to bring the crowd around to his way of thinking. This is a crucial trait for anyone who wants to be a president or leader, and it came naturally to him.

A sports lover, Woodrow played many different types, with a special love for baseball. In fact, he became the president of the baseball association at his school and, later, college. He was also the head editor of his school paper, proving that whatever he tried, he quickly rose to the top.

After high school, Wilson began studying law at Princeton. Again, this came very naturally to him. He was so good that he ended up teaching there and did the same at Cornell University later.

Wilson taught for many years, and during this time, he met his wife-to-be, Ellen Axson. They went on to have three daughters together and, by all accounts, had a very happy marriage.

By 1890, Wilson had returned to Princeton, only this time as a professor. His salary was more than comfortable, but he yearned to keep improving himself. During his time at Princeton, Wilson had many books published, with most of his focus on political science and history. One of the books he wrote, The State, was used by colleges all over America up until the 1920s.

Twelve years after returning to Princeton as a professor, the board at the college promoted him to their president. It was the first time Wilson would use such a title, but it wouldn't be the last. This taste of leadership awakened something in him, and he knew that politics was where he wanted to be.

Wilson ran Princeton for another decade but decided to move on when the chance to become governor of New Jersey arose. He entered the running in 1910 and won with a massive 50,000 votes compared to the 10,000 or so of his opponent.

When Woodrow Wilson became governor of New Jersey, he was 55. Some believed he was too old to rise any higher in politics, so the rest of his journey to the top came as a big shock to them. Actually, there has probably never been a jump in American politics that has been as high and in such a short space of time.

The 1912 American election was wild, with infighting and bickering at a level never seen before then. The Republican Party fell apart under this pressure, and the newly promoted candidate, Woodrow Wilson, took full advantage. His campaign was quick and simple, which caught the American public's imagination. They wanted calm, and Wilson seemed to offer it.

Woodrow Wilson had only been named governor of New Jersey in 1910, and two years later, he won the election for the American presidency! It was incredible, and it all happened so fast that people were still in shock as he was sworn in. Wilson didn't care, though. He was the 28th president of the United States, and he had work to do.

The first two years of his presidency weren't nice. Wilson lost his wife and saw the outbreak of World War I. America wanted no part of a war that was only really affecting Europe, and Wilson promised the public that he would keep the troops home. This promise ensured him a second term in the White House, and he was reelected in 1916.

Unfortunately, World War I had gotten out of control, and many millions had already died. Wilson made the decision in 1917 to send troops over in an attempt to bring an end to the conflict. It worked, and the US helped join forces with their Allies* and finish one of the bloodiest wars in history.

While so many of America's men were away fighting in Europe, women's rights grew in popularity. Women's suffrage* really took hold, and the ladies of America were showing the rest of the world that they were just as smart and important as any man.

Amazingly, it has only been in recent history that women have as many rights as men, and there are still places in the world where they don't. Thankfully, things are still improving, but we have a long way to go.

One of Woodrow's most significant acts as president was the signing of the Treaty of Versailles on June 28, 1919. This was an agreement of peace between the Allies and the Germans and the official end to World War I. Another world war would break out 19 years later, so it seemed that humanity hadn't learned its lesson.

Wilson stepped down from the presidency in 1921 after two terms. His health had already started to fade, and it would worsen in the years following his retirement.

He died on February 3, 1924, at the age of 67, and will always be remembered as the president who stepped in and stopped World War I. He may not have been a war hero or a national champion in wrestling like Abe Lincoln, but Woodrow Wilson deserves his place on any list of amazing presidents.

DWIGHT D. EISENHOWER

SERVED AS PRESIDENT	AGE AT INAUGURATION	PRESIDENT NUMBER
1953-1961	62	34TH
PARTY	**NICKNAME**	**HOMETOWN**
REPUBLICAN	IKE	DENISON, TEXAS

BIOGRAPHY

After taking over from Harry S. Truman, Dwight Eisenhower became the president who oversaw the Cold War and helped create a massive burst of economic growth in America. He was a war hero and as American as apple pie. But one of his most important contributions to history sometimes gets overlooked: Dwight Eisenhower was also the president who pushed America into the Space Race, which eventually put a human being on the moon.

Born on October 14, 1890, as the third of seven sons, Dwight Eisenhower grew up in a very energetic and outgoing family. He also developed a love of books and education, with a special passion for history. His mother —who was against war in all its forms—had a huge collection of history books. Dwight read them repeatedly, often getting lost in what he found in the pages.

Besides history, Dwight also topped his class in math, spelling, debate, and reading. His schoolwork and grades were vitally important, and his parents were stringent on this. They believed in rules and discipline. In fact, all of the Eisenhower boys were given several daily chores that they had to complete, and strong punishments were handed down if standards weren't met.

Young Eisenhower enjoyed the structure of his childhood, and this was something he carried into his later life in the army. He thrived on rules and regulations but also on rewards for hard work.

When he injured his leg in his first year in high school, Eisenhower was told by doctors that he would need to have it amputated or else he would die. His love of sports and the outdoors trumped his fear, and Dwight told them he would rather take the risk and fight the infection. In the end, he recovered and kept his leg. It was a very risky decision, but Eisenhower was a fighter by nature.

His family might not have been wealthy, but they weren't what would be considered destitute, either. Although some prestigious colleges were chasing him, Dwight had always been destined for the military. The organization and structure would have definitely appealed to him.

In 1911, Eisenhower got his wish and enrolled in the American Army. He trained hard and graduated from the Military Academy four years later, just as World War I broke out in Europe. As we know, America originally declared that it wouldn't participate in the war. In fact, this promise had been a big part of Woodrow Wilson's campaign to get voted in for a second term. Eisenhower agreed with President Wilson's decision, but he was more than ready to fight if America decided to change its mind.

They did, and on April 4, 1917, the US declared that they would become part of World War I. Eisenhower begged his superiors to send him overseas as he knew his organization and tactics would be vital in stopping the Germans. He didn't get his wish right away, which annoyed him. By the time he was shipped over to France in February of 1918, the war was dying down. Still, the army saw his potential, and he was handpicked as a future leader.

Almost immediately after his return to the States, Eisenhower was promoted from captain to major. This was a position he would hold with honor for over 16 years. During this time, he would amaze his bosses and fellow soldiers with his tank crew training, organization skills, warfare tactics, and new ideas.

He was selected to attend the Command and General Staff College at Fort Leavenworth, where he graduated at the top of his class.

By 1942, World War II had already been destroying Europe for four years. Unlike in World War I, Eisenhower was now an experienced major. He was shipped over to Europe in June of 1942 with orders to bring the Allies together and organize all of the American troops.

He was named Supreme Commander of the Allied Forces in North Africa, and he quickly advanced his armies on Italy and took down their fascist regime led by Benito Mussolini. It was a massive step toward ending the war and a relief for so much of Europe, which had been living in fear.

Eisenhower continued his steady rise after World War II, and in 1950 he was named Supreme Commander of NATO*. Although that title sounds like something from Star Wars, it is genuinely one of the most important roles in the world. Eisenhower had been entrusted with the safety of the world, and he took that job very seriously.

When the American presidential election came around in 1952, Eisenhower was the heavy favorite. As we know, then-president Harry Truman didn't even bother running against Eisenhower. He knew what the outcome would be, and he was right. Eisenhower won easily, and he was named the 34th president of the United States.

His time in the White House was nearly overshadowed by the Cold War. For years, it seemed that every American feared that their neighbor might be a Communist, and the rivalry between America and the Soviet Union (Russia) was intense. This was never more serious than with the Space Race. Both nations' desperate attempts to put a human being on the moon cost billions of dollars, and the race lasted over a decade.

As president, Eisenhower signed an agreement to form the National Aeronautics and Space Administration—or NASA, its more popular name! Space toys, board games, science fiction books, TV shows, and comics—it seemed that everything popular at the time revolved around space travel, and President Eisenhower was the person who set it off!

In a cruel twist of fate, Dwight Eisenhower died shortly before Neil Armstrong walked on the moon. He never got to see his nation win the Space Race, as he passed away on March 28, 1969, four months before Apollo 11 successfully landed on the moon.

But the Space Race was only part of his legacy. Eisenhower served two terms in office, overseeing the birth of the Cold War and huge growth in American wealth. In the 1950s, America became the most popular country in the world, and kids from every other nation dreamed of eating cheeseburgers at colorful diners, drinking Coca-Cola, going to drive-ins, and everything Hollywood.

Eisenhower was popular from the moment he ran until the day he stepped down in 1961. He was a decorated major in the army and a true American hero.

BARACK OBAMA

SERVED AS PRESIDENT	AGE AT INAUGURATION	PRESIDENT NUMBER
2009-2017	47	44TH
PARTY	**NICKNAME**	**HOMETOWN**
DEMOCRATS	BARRY	HONOLULU, HAWAII

BIOGRAPHY

It is far too easy for us to label Barack Obama as simply the first Black president of the United States. He was so much more, and he came to power in America because he was a very intelligent human being and someone who wanted to always do better for the people of the world. In his time, he fought for LGBTQ+ rights, created the Affordable Care Act, and brought America through one of the worst recessions* in history. He broke down barriers, yes, but he did it by being one of the greatest American presidents of all time, not because of the color of his skin.

Barack Obama was born in Honolulu, Hawaii, on August 4, 1961. His family wasn't well-off, and his mother was very young when she had him. He was raised to believe that none of that stuff should ever hold him back and that education could make any person great if they were dedicated to everything they did. This upbringing and belief helped shape Barack Obama into the amazing person we know him as today.

Obama's childhood was hectic at times, and his father left the family to study at Harvard when Barack was only two. He only saw him once more during a quick visit eight years later. Barack moved to Indonesia with his mother at the age of six to live with her new partner, a student named Lolo Soetoro.

While in Indonesia, Barack's baby sister Maya was born, and he lived a modest life with her, his mom, and his stepfather. He attended a few different schools while there, always excelling in any classes he attended. When he returned to Hawaii in 1971 at age 10, he split his time between his parents' new place and his grandparents' apartment.

Barack Obama was a brilliant student who asked questions and always wanted to know more. He topped his class in most subjects but had a real love of political science. In 1979, he graduated from Punahou School and then moved to Los Angeles after getting accepted into the modest but highly respected Occidental College.

He spent two years there before getting into Columbia University in New York, where he graduated in 1983 with a bachelor's degree in political science. He might not have known it then, but by studying this subject, young Barack was already on the path to becoming president of the United States!

Obama stayed in New York for another few years, reading endless streams of literature, mainly philosophy. He found fun in broadening his mind, and it allowed him to see the world differently. This helped him become the caring man who led his country years later, as it gave him a wider perspective.

His next step was a move to Harvard University, where he unsurprisingly studied law! Of course, we know by now that this is often a crucial step for anyone who wants to become president one day.

This time in his life would give him the tools he would need to move into politics and meet the love of his life, Michelle Robinson! His soon-to-be wife was a very talented lawyer at the time, and they married three years later, in 1992.

After earning his law degree, the Obamas moved to Chicago, and Barack made his move into politics straight away, joining the Democratic Party. His early work included creating Project Vote, a move that earned thousands of African American votes for Bill Clinton. Everyone could already see that Barack Obama had a natural ability to be successful in politics!

Obama was elected to the Senate in 1996, only four years after his move to Chicago. He seemed to have found his home in politics, and his rise was nothing short of a miracle. His big aims were to stop government officials from wasting money and make medical care more readily available to everyone. He also made big changes in how people could receive welfare, meaning the less fortunate people were not so oppressed anymore.

All of this made him extremely popular, and he was promoted as someone who could one day run for office. Barack felt the same way and announced his intention to enter the presidential elections in 2007.

Like some people on this list, his rise from announcing he would run to actually winning was swift. His speeches and public appearances at this time were mind-blowing, and his passion shone through when he was on stage. The people loved him and saw that he wanted only the best for America, which is always a great strength to have.

Between 2007 and being sworn in on January 20, 2009, Barack Obama won not only the votes but the trust of the American people. His victory in the elections did not come as a shock, which is probably the best part of all. It meant that people were voting with their heads and not through their hatred.

Obama went straight to work, announcing fairer rights for the LGBTQ+ community and promising better healthcare for more people. He also brought America closer to the rest of the world, easing tensions with the likes of Egypt, Russia, and Cuba.

He won the Nobel Peace Prize in 2009 for his peace efforts, something which seemed to embarrass him more so than make him happy. He was proud, of course, but people like Barack Obama do good for the world because they want to, not for reward. It is what makes them truly great.

When Barack Obama was sworn in for a second term in 2013, nobody was surprised. His first term had been challenging, but he'd seen America through one of the worst recessions in history. He had made medical care cheaper, helped out those less fortunate with better welfare, and made peace with many nations.

These are the traits that we need to remember when we think of Barack Obama's time in office. He was selfless, brave, and someone who always thought of others before himself.

Barack Obama still strives to help the world today. Alongside his wonderful wife, Michelle Obama, they have spent their whole lives trying to do good for everyone else. I think we can all learn something from that!

RONALD REAGAN

SERVED AS PRESIDENT	AGE AT INAUGURATION	PRESIDENT NUMBER
1981-1989	69	40TH
PARTY	**NICKNAME**	**HOMETOWN**
REPUBLICAN	THE GREAT COMMUNICATOR	TAMPICO, ILLINOIS

BIOGRAPHY

The man who would become known as the "Great Communicator" was not only a popular president, but he was also a former actor who starred in 53 movies! He was the president who saw the end of the Cold War and the Berlin Wall being torn down and nearly destroyed America through a national debt like no other!

By the end of it all, he had finished his time in office with one of the highest approval ratings of all time!

Ronald Reagan was born in Tampico, Illinois, on February 6, 1911. For the first eight years of his life, the Reagan family moved around a lot, and it wasn't until 1919 that they returned to Tampico and settled down properly for the first time. This stability gave young Ronald a chance to really concentrate on his education, and he took the opportunity with both hands.

At a time when racial hatred was almost seen as normal in many parts of America, Ronald Reagan was known as the kid who despised any form of discrimination. He believed in equal rights, even as a child. His parents were of Irish and Scottish descent, and their Catholic beliefs had been passed down to their son. Reagan's family rightly believed that everyone was born the same, and this was something he tried to promote throughout his life.

The Reagans were not a wealthy family, and Ronald attended mainly public schools. Despite this, he managed to stand out in politics, sports, and acting, starring in many school plays in his youth. His grades were always high, earning him a place at Eureka College in Illinois. Here, his stance on civil rights grew, and he always tried to show his support for minorities and those who didn't have the opportunities afforded to him.

After graduating from Eureka, he worked as a sports announcer before moving to Hollywood in 1937 to pursue a career in acting!

His time in the movies was a success. Reagan wasn't one of Hollywood's biggest stars, but he was well-known and pretty popular. The experiences he got from being in front of the camera ended up helping him in his political campaigns years later, although he had no plans of being in politics at the time. Reagan soon discovered that public speaking came naturally to him, and this charm earned him the nickname of the "Great Communicator."

In 1952, he decided to help a fellow actor, Helen Gahagan Douglas, run for the U.S. Senate. She was up against future-president Richard Nixon. The campaign was a failure, but Reagan found that he had a knack for politics. He quickly decided to separate himself from Helen and concentrate on his own political career, but not before building his experience by helping some other campaigns along the way.

Eight years after his unsuccessful support of Helen Gahagan Douglas's Senate campaign, he switched alliances and supported Richard Nixon, who was now running for the American presidency. Reagan gave over 200 speeches for Nixon, but his team lost again. Nixon was not a likable candidate, which is probably why he had the very lovable and charismatic Ronald Reagan make his speeches! Also, he had been running against

America's favorite son, John F. Kennedy, so he never really had a chance.

Throughout all of this, Ronald Reagan continued to make movies. They were less frequent, and he made his last appearance on a Hollywood screen as Jack Browning in the 1964 crime film, The Killers. After that, he decided to concentrate solely on politics and his attempts at winning the American presidency.

By the time he was 55, Ronald Reagan had yet to really make a mark in politics. When he ran for the position of governor of California in 1966, most people mocked his lack of experience. He wowed them with his public speaking, though, and shocked everyone when he won.

Once in power, he maintained his popularity, and it started to grow. His speeches and promises continued to gather more supporters every year. He was reelected and remained governor of California for 10 years, He used this time to strengthen his campaign to run for the American presidency, and the public became more and more supportive.

Reagan swore that he would lower taxes, which is always a good move when someone wants to win the people over! They didn't care how he planned to do it and only listened to what they wanted to hear. By the time the 1980 elections came around, the American people wanted Ronald Reagan as their next president.

He won and took office in January of 1981. He was 69 years old.

Two months into his time in the White House, Reagan was shot as he left a hotel in Washington. He nearly died but became the first American president in history to survive an assassination attempt while in office. His speech after leaving the hospital, in which he claimed God had spared him, made him even more popular. His approval rating at the time was 73% and is still regarded as one of the largest ever recorded.

Reagan's promises that taxes would be lowered came true, but underneath it all, he was making things harder for the less wealthy. They all had jobs now, but the pay was so low that they couldn't really survive on it. He left a massive national debt after he stepped down from the presidency, and a lot of these decisions are still questioned today.

Despite all of this, he easily won a second election in 1984 and quickly made it his mission to clamp down on the illegal drugs that had started to flood the streets. By the eighties, drug use in America was at an all-time high, and it was becoming more dangerous because of it. Reagan failed in that particular mission, but at least he brought the problem to the public's attention.

The end of Ronald Reagan's second term in office saw the fall of the Berlin Wall in 1989, which had separated East and West Germany since 1961. It was one of the most important moments in German and European history, and it was also the beginning of the end of the Cold War.

When Ronald Reagan stepped down in 1989 and handed the presidency over to George W. Bush, he did so as one of the most popular presidents in American history. Many of his decisions while in office might have been questionable, but his charm will forever be remembered and cherished.

JOHN F. KENNEDY

SERVED AS PRESIDENT	AGE AT INAUGURATION	PRESIDENT NUMBER
1961-1963	43	35TH

PARTY	NICKNAME	HOMETOWN
DEMOCRATS	JFK	BROOKLINE, MASSACHUSETTS

BIOGRAPHY

John F. Kennedy. JFK. Jack. America's favorite son. There are many ways our next president was referred to over the years, but none can explain just how loved the man was and continues to be. JFK is possibly the most famous American president of all time and certainly one of the most important. His work for civil rights and his eventual assassination have left him forever imprinted on the memories of the nation and even the world. He was a great president and a wonderful human being.

If someone wanted to make the ideal American president in a lab, they would probably end up with something like a JFK clone. His looks, attitude, charisma, and upbringing all scream a picture-perfect leader. He could speak eloquently and wow a crowd, and he was tough when he needed to be. More than anything, people trusted him.

John Fitzgerald Kennedy was born on May 29, 1917, in Brookline, Massachusetts, to Joseph and Rose. His father was a politician, and his mother was a highly respected philanthropist. The Kennedys were an extremely political family from top to bottom, and it always seemed that JFK was destined to become a president.

His younger brother, Robert, would also become an influential politician and lawyer. Unfortunately, that wasn't the only similarity he had with JFK. Robert—or "Bobby" as he was known—was also assassinated later in life.

Through his family's wealth and connections, JFK was

given the best education. The subjects that interested him most early on were history and politics. He also loved sports, playing football for his high school in Boston.

Despite his regular exercise and fitness, JFK suffered from many health problems in his youth, being hospitalized more than once. At first, it was thought he had leukemia, but it was later found to be colitis. After that, JFK seemed to look at life differently. He wanted to make the most of it, and such a scare can often affect a person, especially one so young.

JFK attended Harvard University after high school, receiving a Bachelor of Arts in government. His thesis on the reasons why England was so unprepared for World War II was so good that it was published as a book. He called it Why England Slept, and it quickly became a bestseller. It also catapulted him into the public eye.

Kennedy always had a way with words, which he used in writing his speeches later in life when he campaigned for the presidency.

After Harvard, JFK planned on attending Yale Law School, but his plans were cut short. With World War II getting out of control, JFK enrolled in the U.S. Navy, hoping to go overseas and help in the fight. While there, a torpedo attack by the Japanese cut his boat in half. Kennedy led a rescue party, dragging one crewmate to safety by clenching a strap between his teeth and swimming him to shore.

His war efforts, best-selling book, good looks, and charm meant that he would end up going into politics after the war. Even though he was still very young, JFK ran for the position of U.S. Senator in 1953. He won and was reelected six years later after a stellar performance.

Throughout all of this, JFK struggled with back problems. Much of the time, when he was being seen in public with a proud smile across his face, he was actually in severe agony. He hid it, as he knew the people wanted someone who was seen almost as a superhero to lead them.

In 1955, his back problems became too much, and he was forced to have a second operation to try and fix it. He didn't waste his time during his recovery, and he wrote another book, Profiles in Courage, from his bed. It not only outsold his first book but also won him the most prestigious prize in literature: the Pulitzer Prize.

During his three terms as senator, JFK met a young woman named Jacqueline Bouvier. "Jackie," as she became known to the public, was beautiful. With JFK being so handsome, they became something of a celebrity couple before there was such a thing as a celebrity couple! Instead of damaging his popularity, the marriage put him on the cover of every newspaper and magazine, and the public took the Kennedys into their hearts.

JFK made his move for the American presidency in 1960, publicly declaring that he would run in the next election. Most other candidates didn't take him seriously, believing him to be far too young, but they had underestimated just how popular he was among the people.

His election battle with Richard Nixon was seen as something of a Beauty and the Beast fight to the death! Nixon was hard-edged and grumpy, while JFK was charming and a believer in civil rights. In the end, the people spoke, and JFK became the youngest president in the history of the United States on January 20, 1961.

Within a month at the White House, he ordered the U.S. troops to invade Cuba. The Bay of Pigs* was worldwide news, proving that JFK wasn't just a pretty face. He could make the hard decisions too.

JFK also came into power just as the Space Race was really heating up. His promise that America would put a man on the moon before the end of the decade was widely laughed at, but it came true. The saddest part was that the man himself didn't live to see it.

Although his time as president was tragically brief, JFK made a lot of strides forward. His creation of the Peace Corps was incredible, and there was now an organization whose sole purpose was to help those less fortunate around the globe. He also made many speeches supporting civil rights for the African American community, and he openly demanded that America start to treat minorities much better.

At a time when the Cold War was at its most intense, JFK managed to cool tensions and avoid what would have been a catastrophic nuclear war. He put an end to the Cuban Missile Crisis*and brought a level of peace to the minds of the American people that had been missing since World War II.

Sadly, JFK was only president for two years. During a public visit to Dallas on November 22, 1963, he was shot by Lee Harvey Oswald as he rode in an open-topped car with his wife. It was one of America's darkest days, and the term "I remember where I was when the news came through" was born.

He left behind two beautiful children and a gaping hole in America's heart when he died. His murder was senseless and started a chain reaction of other assassinations that continued to rock the nation.

JFK tops most lists of great presidents, as he was such a great man. We will never know what he might have achieved if he'd lived, and we can only leave that to our imagination. But we should always remember him as someone who believed in the same rights for everyone, regardless of the color of their skin.

LYNDON B. JOHNSON

SERVED AS PRESIDENT	AGE AT INAUGURATION	PRESIDENT NUMBER
1963-1969	55	36TH
PARTY	NICKNAME	HOMETOWN
DEMOCRATS	LBJ	STONEWALL, TEXAS

BIOGRAPHY

The man who stepped into the presidency after the assassination of John F. Kennedy is often overlooked simply because he had to take over from JFK, one of the most popular presidents in history. But Lyndon Johnson's time in office was as eventful as anyone else's. His signature on the Civil Rights Act of 1964 paved the way for more equality for minorities, and on the flip side, many of his decisions escalated the Vietnam War. Of course, his place in time will always live in the shade of JFK's reputation, but few presidents would ever shine under such a large shadow!

Lyndon Johnson was born on August 27, 1908, in Stonewall, Texas. His parents didn't have much money and raised their kids with strict religious beliefs. They were fine people who tried to always do right by others, and they passed this down to Lyndon. Life wasn't easy, but they worked hard and made the most of it.

At school, young Lyndon was an energetic and talkative child. He was known as someone who could entertain a crowd and was named class president in the 11th grade. He enjoyed baseball, debate, and public speaking and maintained high grades throughout his schooling.

When his parents pressured him to go to college, he caved, but his time there didn't last. Johnson left Southwest Texas Junior College after only a few months and moved to California. While there, he met up with his cousin, who owned a law firm, and asked if he could work there. He soon learned the tricks of the trade but still found himself thinking about politics, which had always intrigued him.

After saving some money, Johnson moved back to Texas and enrolled in Texas State. He studied political science and history and used his spare time to teach Mexican American children who couldn't afford—or simply weren't allowed to attend—public school. Segregation* was still rampant in Texas, so the wealthier college students often shunned Johnson. He never let it bother him, though, as he knew he was doing the right thing.

The discrimination he saw in his college years spurred him on to try and earn a position where he could make a difference. Johnson didn't like what he saw and could not understand why people were being denied an education simply because of the color of their skin.

After Texas State, Johnson became a high school teacher. He loved his job, but working at the local schools opened his eyes more to the discrimination he saw. He knew that if he wanted to make a real difference, he would have to move into politics and do it himself.

On April 10, 1937, Lyndon Johnson became a congressman in Texas. It was a powerful position but still a surprise to some, given his lack of Ivy League education. He worked extremely hard and managed to stay in power for five more elections. Maintaining the public's trust for so long was an impressive thing to do, and it showed the dedication and passion he possessed.

By 1940, America had been dragged into World War II, and in June of that year, Lyndon Johnson was given the rank of lieutenant commander in the U.S. Navy. He was personally selected for this role by Franklin D. Roosevelt, as the two men had become close in the previous years.

In the years following the war, Johnson continued to climb in politics. He made connections, and the trust shown in him by FDR gave him credit with the public. In 1948, he was elected to the U.S. Senate, quickly making a name for himself as someone who would give their all for the cause.

Johnson stayed in the Senate for many years and was promoted to Senate minority leader in 1953, making him the youngest person in history to be given that particular honor. It seemed that even though he had been a bit of a latecomer to politics, Lyndon Johnson was set to make it to the top!

When John F. Kennedy won the election in 1960, everyone thought that his opponent, Richard Nixon, would be given the vice presidency. It went to a vote instead, and Lyndon Johnson was sworn in as JFK's right-hand man. Both men were passionate about civil rights, and the two of them coming together was a vitally important moment in time. Without Lyndon Johnson stepping in when tragedy took JFK from the world a few years later, who knows what would have happened to the civil rights movement?

Unfortunately, tragedy did strike. After the assassination of JFK in Dallas, Lyndon Johnson was sworn in on November 22, 1963. The following year, he signed the Civil Rights Act that had been put in place by JFK. It was hoped that the new laws would put an end to horrific things such as segregation and discrimination. There was still a lot of work to do, but Johnson's signing of the Civil Rights Act was a huge step forward.

In August 1964, Johnson made a decision to send more American troops into Vietnam. Instead of forcing the opposition to lay down their weapons as he had hoped, the move only added fuel to the fire. Tensions in Vietnam rose higher than they'd ever been, and the war escalated to unknown heights. His decision had really backfired, and much of the public turned on him.

The rest of his time in office was mainly dominated by the war in Vietnam. It is easy to forget just how tense things were in America in the 1960s, but Lyndon Johnson played a big part in keeping it as calm as possible. His choices regarding the war in Vietnam were questionable at best, but the Civil Rights Act was a monumental moment not just in American history but that of the human race.

After his two terms, Johnson declared live on television that he would not be running for a third. He was replaced by Richard Nixon, who would show the Americans that having a calm and reliable president such as Lyndon Johnson in charge wasn't exactly as bad as all that!

When Lyndon Johnson died on January 22, 1973, he seemed to be instantly remembered as the man who steered America into war in Vietnam. In truth, the US had been getting dragged in long before he sent the troops. He will also always be referred to as the president who stepped in after John F. Kennedy was assassinated, but it had been expected that Johnson would have been elected as president at some stage, even if JFK had seen out his terms.

All in all, Lyndon Johnson wasn't perfect, but none of us are. He made some mistakes in his time in office, but he made many positive changes too!

BILL CLINTON

SERVED AS PRESIDENT	AGE AT INAUGURATION	PRESIDENT NUMBER
1993-2001	46	42ND

PARTY	NICKNAME	HOMETOWN
DEMOCRATS	COMEBACK KID	HOPE, ARKANSAS

BIOGRAPHY

One of the more recent presidents on our list, and certainly one of the most popular, is Bill Clinton. Despite some major public embarrassments, he left the White House after two terms with a 68% approval rating. He was every woman's dream guy and every man's best friend. Bill Clinton was the classic American president and the first since JFK to catch the public's attention in such a way.

Born William Jefferson Blythe III on August 19, 1946, Bill grew up never knowing his birth father. William Blythe II died three months before Bill was born, leaving the family penniless and alone. Bill's mother, Virginia Kelley, needed a career, and she decided to put her son in the care of his grandparents in Hope, Arkansas, while she traveled to Virginia to study nursing.

During this period, Bill saw the full effects of racial segregation, which was still evident in Arkansas. His grandparents ran a small grocery store and regularly gave credit to people of any color despite many other local businesses refusing to do the same. Their views had a massive effect on Bill, who quickly saw that racial hatred and discrimination were pointless and wrong.

When Virginia returned to Hope after her nurse training, she met and married Roger Clinton. Although Bill used his new stepfather's surname in his youth, he didn't legally adopt it until he was 15. Later in life, Bill spoke of his childhood around this period as a scary one. Roger Clinton was violent and abusive to Bill, his brother, and his mother, and Bill claimed that he had to step in to stop the abuse more than once.

During his high school years, he did well in English, social studies, music, and debate. In fact, it was the last of these that really caught his attention. Following a mock trial set up by his teacher, Bill claims that he caught the political bug. He fell in love with the idea of public speaking, debating, and how the court system worked.

Two other significant moments that influenced Bill in his youth were a trip to the White House and a televised speech he saw by Martin Luther King Junior. The first of these was when the Boys Nation* visited the White House to meet John F. Kennedy. Bill said later that he was in awe of the man, and the idea of being in the same position one day greatly appealed to him. The second was Martin Luther King's famous "I have a dream" speech, which is still just as powerful today. If you haven't heard it, then check it out on YouTube!

Bill's college life started at Oxford, but he soon moved to Yale. He wanted to study law, and Yale was considered one of the best law schools in America. While there, he met his future wife, Hillary, who would become an extraordinarily successful and well-respected politician herself.

After practicing law for a few years, Bill decided it was time to move into politics. He wasn't always successful and had several setbacks before he found his feet. In 1978, he ran for governor of Arkansas and won. He had lost the same election a couple of years earlier, but he never let things like that stop him from chasing his dream. Sometimes, the defeats in our life become the most important, as they teach us how to lose and how to bounce back even higher.

His new role meant that he was the youngest-ever governor of Arkansas, and he performed brilliantly. He quickly built up a reputation as someone who got things done, and his people skills were what set him apart. Anyone who talked to Bill Clinton felt like they had just spoken with greatness, and it was this charisma that helped him succeed in politics so quickly.

In his ten years as governor of Arkansas, Bill made massive changes to the education and medical systems in the area. He believed that the less wealthy classes needed more support if they were to flourish, and he was right. Having come from a struggling family, Bill knew how hard it could be to live that way.

When the presidential election buzz started in the early 1990s, Bill announced he would run. Much of the public didn't even know who he was at the time, and when they heard his age, they were surprised. He was going up against the strict but respected George W. Bush, who had an 80% approval rating, so he wasn't given much of a chance. That meant Bill had to win over most of the country simply by using his intelligence and charm.

Amazingly, he achieved this in such a short time and won over the American voters. The whole world seemed to fall in love with him.

Bill instantly made the Family and Medical Leave Act a law. This meant that people could now take the required time away from work to deal with things like serious illness, pregnancy, and early childcare. It was a huge step and something that cemented his place in the public's hearts.

During his time as president, America saw the longest streak of economic growth in its history. Unemployment was at its lowest in 30 years, and education and grades had improved dramatically. He increased the number of police officers on the streets, creating new jobs and bringing the crime rate down.

By 1996, Bill was untouchable. The election that year was a no-contest, and Bill was expected to win from the beginning. He did—easily—but it wasn't all a dream for him during his second term in office.

In 1998, the Monica Lewinsky trial became worldwide news. In a time before the internet, every newspaper, magazine, and news channel showed nothing but the Bill Clinton scandal for months on end. Lewinsky had claimed Bill had had an affair with her, and the media were relentless.

Incredibly, his popularity stayed the same despite how the newspapers tried to destroy his reputation. There were even calls for him to run for a third term, and his approval rating showed that he certainly would have won.

He didn't run, but he is still very influential in politics today. Bill continues to raise awareness and influence others.

Since his time in office, Bill Clinton has set up many charities and fundraising events and has given hundreds of speeches promoting better education for the masses. He continues to do good, and he's never lost that little boy inside who came from nothing to reach the White House. Bill Clinton will always be among the most popular American presidents, and he was also one of the most successful.

CALVIN COOLIDGE

SERVED AS PRESIDENT	AGE AT INAUGURATION	PRESIDENT NUMBER
1923-1929	51	30TH

PARTY	NICKNAME	HOMETOWN
REPUBLICAN	SILENT CAL	PLYMOUTH NOTCH, VERMONT

BIOGRAPHY

If Bill Clinton was a swashbuckling president who wowed the nation with his charm, then Calvin Coolidge was the opposite in that regard. He became known as "Silent Cal" due to his reserved nature, and his rise to the top was more like a steady stream than a dam bursting! Still, he achieved a lot in his time in the White House and proved that you don't need to be suave and brash to be president.

John Calvin Coolidge Jr. was born in Vermont on July 4, 1872, making him the only American president to be born on Independence Day! Although he had been christened John after his father, he was called Calvin his whole life.

His father was a respected businessman who dabbled in local politics. The Coolidge family was quite well-off, so education was always there for the kids. Calvin took full advantage, reading as much as he could and studying hard at school. He found that philosophy really interested him, and he liked the idea of several perspectives on one subject or issue. During his high school years, he also excelled in debate.

Calvin's mother died when he was 12, which affected him greatly. Around this time, his sister also passed away, and his father remarried. Despite these heartbreaks, he continued to work hard in his education, with his father always edging him toward law.

Coolidge took a job as a lawyer's apprentice, hoping to

learn the trade that way rather than attending an expensive law school. It worked, and through strict saving during his apprenticeship, he was soon able to afford a small office of his own. He opened his practice in Massachusetts and quickly earned a name for being hard-working and loyal to his clients.

When he was only 24, Coolidge got involved in the presidential campaign of William McKinley, helping out in the campaign offices and studying the process. With his new law practice and his time spent campaigning, he was a busy man, but he seemed to thrive under such circumstances.

In 1906, Coolidge moved into politics, serving in the Massachusetts House of Representatives. He used his position of power to help fight for women's suffrage and became known for being dependable. Coolidge was becoming the kind of politician people felt they could trust.

Five years after being brought into the House of Representatives, he found himself being encouraged to run for Senate. The vote was a landslide, and he was promoted in 1911. It was a huge step for someone so new to politics, but still not a surprise, given his stellar reputation.

Coolidge's rise continued, and in 1918, he was named governor of Massachusetts. Although this was a huge honor for him, he only stayed in that position for two years. Another job was calling to him, and it was one he couldn't turn down.

After barely any campaigning, Coolidge was named vice president to Warren G. Harding and sworn in on March

4, 1921. The election of both men had come as a bit of a shock, but America wanted stability after World War I. During this period, he earned the nickname "Silent Cal" due to his quiet approach to life outside of the White House.

With many lavish parties, plays, and social events to attend because of his new position, Coolidge always seemed uncomfortable in such settings. Although he was an outstanding public speaker, he preferred to be left to his thoughts in private. The nickname and jokes regarding his quietness never seemed to bother him, though.

Following the shocking death of Warren G. Harding while still in office on August 2, 1923, Calvin Coolidge was sworn in as the new president. Harding had been well-liked by the American people, so Coolidge had a fight on his hands to win them over. Thankfully, his quiet nature actually seemed to reassure the public, and they gave him their trust as they had done with Harding.

Coolidge had only been in the White House a year when the next election rolled around. Unlike so many candidates in the past, Coolidge ran a clean campaign. He used no smear tactics and never tried to ridicule his opponents during public speeches. Instead of pointing out everything that was wrong with the other candidates, he told the people what he would do to fix any issues. It was a refreshing approach and one that worked.

Coolidge was voted in for a second term in 1924, and it would be his first and only full one. His time in office was one of calm, which America desperately needed at the time. He made tough decisions when they had to be made, but he did it without looking for praise and fame.

Coolidge helped the economy flourish like it never had before, and the Roaring Twenties was born under his leadership. It was one of the greatest periods in America's history.

When Calvin Coolidge died on January 5, 1933, he was 60. He left behind a legacy that has to be considered one of the most underrated of all time. Maybe this is because he didn't create any scandal or simply because everything went well under his leadership. Whatever the reasons, we should always remember him as a fantastic president who proved that class is something that always shines through, even without all of the over-the-top bravado to back it up.

JAMES K. POLK

SERVED AS PRESIDENT	AGE AT INAUGURATION	PRESIDENT NUMBER
1845-1849	49	11TH

PARTY	NICKNAME	HOMETOWN
DEMOCRATS	YOUNG HICKORY	PINEVILLE, NORTH CAROLINA

President James Polk often gets overlooked, but his reputation has had something of a rebirth in the last few years. Historians have started to give him credit for how he grew America, not just in recognition but in size. They have also noted how he achieved all of this in such a short space of time. In fact, in his four years in charge, the United States had its largest period of expansion in its history.

James Knox Polk was born in Pineville, North Carolina, on November 2, 1795. He was the first of ten children, and his family was of average wealth and made up mainly of farmers. They had emigrated from Scotland not long before James's birth, and the Polk clan was known as an authoritative group who took charge wherever they went.

In fact, after James's father moved with four of his adult children to Duck River (now Maury County, Tennessee), he quickly forced his way into the small local senate. He became the most influential politician in the area and regularly had aspiring president Andrew Jackson over for dinner. It is said that young James Polk found his love for politics at these social gatherings, and he tried everything from then on to be just like his new hero, Andrew Jackson.

Polk was sickly as a child, which was extremely challenging for a kid in the 19th century. At a time when physical strength was seen as far more important than education, there was always a chance of a weaker child being left behind. Fortunately for Polk, the doctors managed to help him, and he recovered over time. It took a while, but soon Polk was as strong and fit as the rest of his brothers.

Despite his family's farming traditions, Polk was soon dreaming of a different type of career. He studied hard between his daily chores, and when the chance to enroll at the University of North Carolina came, he gratefully took it. Polk studied debate and law and graduated with top marks in 1818.

Following his time in college, Polk moved to Nashville to begin a career as an attorney. Of course, law was always the path he would choose because, well, that seems to be the way for American presidents, right?

Polk practiced law for five years before edging his way into politics in 1823. He did this by joining the local militia and rapidly rising through the ranks. He had a knack for leading and found organizing his men easy. Those he commanded respected him, and Polk's name was soon being spoken of as a future leader.

His reputation preceded him, and he was accepted into the House of Representatives at the age of 29! If this wasn't shocking enough, his first speech as a representative blew the roof off the place! He asked that the law be changed so that presidents were voted in by the public and not by the electors*. It might not seem like much, but when the public doesn't get to vote on such matters, the people in power can keep whoever they like in charge for as long as they wish. This is why they were so frightened when Polk gave his speech, as many of the corrupt representatives feared for their jobs.

At 40, Polk had become one of the lead speakers in the House of Representatives. Four years later, he was governor of Texas, although this didn't go as smoothly as the rest of Polk's path through politics. In truth, his views on the abolition of slavery and how much the government was spending caused most of the tension.

His time as governor might have been strained, but Polk still believed he could make it farther. To some, he was too serious in his attitude, and the American people felt distant from him. After a couple of losses in his bid to become vice president, a series of unforeseen events suddenly cast him into the running for an even higher position—the presidency! Polk was still expected to perform poorly, but the public had actually started to see his no-nonsense attitude as charming.

From a failed attempt at becoming vice president to being sworn in as president of the United States on March 4, 1845, things moved really fast for Polk. In his first year in office, America went to war with Mexico. It was a bloody exchange that lasted nearly three years, but by the end of it, America had taken control of California, Texas, Nevada, and Utah. It was a massive expansion and helped shape the America we see on the map today.

The Mexican War (1846–1848) took its toll on Polk, and his health rapidly deteriorated. He might have only served one term as president, but he achieved a lot in that time. Although Polk had spoken out against slavery for many years, he never officially stated that it should be outlawed once he was in power, which is one of his greatest shames. Still, he passed several pieces of legislation* that attempted to set the wheels in motion for the abolition of slavery.

Another of his achievements was restoring the Independent Treasury, which basically lessened the power the banks had over the common people. Before then, America had seen several occasions when the banking system imploded, causing recessions and depressions. Polk wanted the banks to be held accountable, and his Independent Treasury system remained in place until the 1920s.

Polk barely survived his first term in office. In fact, by the time he left the White House, he was struggling to walk. Three months after retiring, Polk was hospitalized. Doctors presumed it to be cholera, and he died in his bed with his wife Sarah by his side. He was only 53.

James K. Polk might only have served one term as president, but in that time, he grew the landmass of America by a substantial amount. He challenged the greedy bankers and made some of the earliest strides in abolishing slavery. He might slip through the cracks of other lists of great presidents, but he deserves his place on this one.

GROVER CLEVELAND

SERVED AS PRESIDENT	AGE AT INAUGURATION	PRESIDENT NUMBER
1885-1889 & 1893-1897	47 & 55	22ND & 24TH
PARTY	NICKNAME	HOMETOWN
DEMOCRATS	GROVER THE GOOD	CALDWELL, NEW JERSEY

BIOGRAPHY

Now, I know what you're thinking. The 22nd and the 24th president; how can that be possible? Well, it happened, and it was as wild as you just imagined! But Grover Cleveland isn't just famous for being the only president to have led for two interrupted terms. He is known for clamping down on corruption among his government officials, modernizing the U.S. Navy, and his brutal honesty.

Stephen Grover Cleveland was born in Caldwell, New Jersey, on March 18, 1837. His father was a well-respected minister, but the family struggled financially. Stephen—or Grover as he was always called—was the fifth of nine children, so the Cleveland family had a lot of mouths to feed. Still, they took whatever education was available to them.

Grover was known as a playful child, always pulling pranks on his brothers and sisters. He was energetic and spent nearly all of his time outside exploring and playing sports. When it came to his studies, they were often interrupted and fractured. The Cleveland kids had to be pulled out of school mid-semester on many occasions, as the family couldn't afford the tuition.

Even through his high school years, Grover was often forced to come home early to tend to an ill family member or take a part-time job to make ends meet. His family really struggled, and it fell on Grover, more often than not, to be the one to keep them going. Despite all of this, he managed to finish college and open his own law firm in 1862, only a year after the Civil War had broken out.

Grover feared he might be drafted, but when he was appointed district attorney of Erie County, he assumed he wouldn't be asked to fight. When Congress passed the Conscription Act of 1863—demanding that any able-bodied men report for duty or hire a replacement—Grover chose the second option. He paid a Polish man, George Benninsky, to go to war for him.

By the time the war had ended, Grover's law firm was flourishing. When he was asked to become the sheriff of Erie County, he accepted. Being sheriff meant getting a foot in the door of politics, and that had long been a dream of his.

Grover committed himself to his new role and stayed in that position for 11 years. He was known for being a strict disciplinarian and someone that demanded the same honesty he gave. When the chance to become mayor of Buffalo arose, everyone expected Grover to be given the job. He was, and he continued to do business in the same no-nonsense manner. The public appreciated how he ran things, as they knew they could trust him, which is a massive plus in politics.

Although his rise through politics had been relatively slow up until that point, it would soon accelerate. Within a year of being named mayor of Buffalo, Grover had been promoted to governor of New York. Again, he quickly hunted down the corrupt members of the board and fired them when they were caught. His reputation grew, and the public believed he was the type of man they needed to run their country instead of just a single state.

Only two years after cleaning up New York, Grover was in the running for the American presidency.

The man he was up against in the elections, James G. Blaine, had a reputation for being corrupt. It was probably for this reason that Grover, a man of honor, was pushed as his opponent. His campaign revolved around this very point, and he used the slogan, "A public office is a public trust." It was a way of saying that Blaine was crooked, and Grover Cleveland was the man to clean the government up.

The campaign worked, and on March 4, 1885, Grover Cleveland was sworn in as the 22nd American president. His first term in office went as planned, and he spent a lot of time getting to the bottom of the corruption that was so rife. Many men were fired, and those who were thinking about cheating the taxpayers quickly changed their minds. Grover downsized all departments and streamlined government spending so that a penny wasn't wasted.

His next step was to modernize the U.S. Navy, which had been slightly lagging when compared to some of the other superpowers, such as Britain and France. Grover wanted everyone else to know that America couldn't be messed with, and his actions worked. With the Navy's weapons and equipment modernized, they were now the major force to be reckoned with!

All of this should have been enough to win him a second term easily, but a nasty smear campaign by his opponent, Benjamin Harrison, turned the public against him. Grover left the White House on March 4, 1889, after just one term, and surely planned never to return.

It only took Benjamin Harrison a couple of years to send America into a massive economic disaster. His crazy spending and corruption had started as soon as his term had begun, and the American people quickly realized what a mistake they'd made. Grover, who had returned to his law practice and a deserved quiet life, must have been thinking, "I told you so."

Instead of letting America wallow in the mess they had made, Grover agreed to run against Harrison once more. This time, Harrison's dirty tactics didn't work, and Grover Cleveland was voted back in for a second term. His first had ended in 1889, but his second didn't begin until 1893!

Again, Grover was set with the task of cleaning up the administration. He achieved his goals once more and led his country out of the mess Harrison had dragged it into. The public realized their mistake, and there were loud calls for Grover to run for a third term. He declined, and William McKinley took over the presidency. (We will discuss him soon!)

After his time in office, Grover retired to his Princeton estate with his wife and six children. He lived a quiet life but often gave speeches on political issues when asked. He died at the age of 71, with his last words being, "I have tried so hard to do right."

He certainly did that. It's just a pity his time in office was interrupted halfway through.

JAMES MADISON

SERVED AS PRESIDENT	AGE AT INAUGURATION	PRESIDENT NUMBER
1809-1817	57	4TH
PARTY	**NICKNAME**	**HOMETOWN**
DEMOCRATIC-REPUBLICAN	FATHER OF THE CONSTITUTION	PORT CONWAY, VIRGINIA

BIOGRAPHY

James Madison was someone who genuinely changed the face of America. Through his passion for his country, he became known as "The Father of the Constitution," and that alone would be enough for anyone's place in history. He was also one of the men who wrote the Bill of Rights and the president that went to war with mighty Great Britain in 1812, all of which make him one of the most influential presidents in history.

James Madison was born on March 16, 1751, in Belle Grove. His family owned vast amounts of land and were successful tobacco farmers. Because of their wealth, James was taught by the most expensive tutors and thrived under their guidance. He excelled in classical languages, mathematics, and geography.

His love of languages continued into early adulthood, and he chose to study Latin, Greek, and theology when he enrolled at Princeton. While there, Madison fell in love with philosophy and everything it had to offer the world. He believed that he became enlightened through it and that his views on the world shifted for the better.

Even with his expensive education, he left Princeton still unsure of what career he wanted. After teaching himself law in his spare time, it was expected that he would open his own firm. Madison resisted, feeling that politics might be more suited to his philosophical way of thinking.

Around this time, he met Thomas Jefferson, and the

soon-to-be 3rd president of America took young Madison under his wing. They studied politics together and shared their views on how they thought their country should be run. Through this connection and Madison's clear intelligence, he was elected to the House of Representatives in 1789.

Only two years after receiving this honor, Madison's father passed away, leaving him multiple acres of land. With the new tobacco fields and the massive house came many slaves, who Madison reportedly saw as "property." His view on slavery is one of the nastiest parts of who he was, but sadly, this backward belief was shared by nearly all of America at the time.

During this period, France and America were at war. After suffering a crippling defeat in modern-day Haiti, French leader Napoleon gave up his idea of a New Empire and accepted defeat. Madison, James Monroe, and Thomas Jefferson were asked to make a deal with the French, and this meeting produced our previously discussed Louisiana Purchase. As we know, this one move literally doubled the size of the United States.

Through moves such as the Louisiana Purchase and his friendship with Thomas Jefferson, Madison made the inevitable next step up in politics when he ran for the presidency in 1808. He faced stiff opposition, but the much-loved Jefferson—who was coming to the end of his second term in office—had vouched for him, which meant a lot to the voters.

The elections were tight, and even after Madison was sworn in on March 4, 1809, some of the Senate were heavily against his appointment.

Madison's first couple of years in charge were pretty uneventful. His dislike of minorities continued to stain his reputation, though, and he made many attempts to push the American Indians farther away from central America. He planned on reintegrating them, but they had never asked to be bothered in the first place. In fact, they got so sick of how they were being treated that they joined up with the English in one last attempt to spark a second War of Independence.

The resulting attack on the White House by the English and the American Indians caused a lot of damage when a fire broke out. The Americans held them off before defeating their opponents, and the victory made Madison even more popular among the people. He was now seen as a war hero, which helped him win the vote for his second term in office.

He stepped down in 1817, making way for the next president on our list, James Monroe. Madison left behind a legacy of American growth and a period in the nation's history when it started to really become the most powerful in the world. Before his time in the White House, he helped create the Bill of Rights and the Constitution, but his views on African Americans and American Indians will always leave a bad taste in our mouths.

Explaining these views away as "just the way people thought back then" does little to take the sting out of it, but it is unfortunately true. To thoroughly understand history, we often have to try and grasp the way people were programmed in that era. Still, the bad things from our past can never be forgotten, and we can only learn from past mistakes and make our present and future better.

JAMES MONROE

SERVED AS PRESIDENT	AGE AT INAUGURATION	PRESIDENT NUMBER
1817-1825	58	5TH
PARTY	**NICKNAME**	**HOMETOWN**
DEMOCRATIC-REPUBLICAN	ERA OF GOOD FEELINGS	WESTMORELAND COUNTY, VIRGINIA

BIOGRAPHY

Along with our previous entrants, James Madison and Thomas Jefferson, James Monroe was one of the people who helped broker the Louisiana Purchase. He became a war hero while still a teenager and was initially against the Constitution. He was one of the Founding Fathers, and during his presidency, he managed to ease long-running tensions between America and the British. James Monroe might be one of the lesser-known presidents, but he is still just as interesting.

Born into a farming family in Monroe Hall, Virginia, on April 28, 1758, James Monroe grew up having to fight for everything he got. Due to his family's lack of money, he could only attend school 11 weeks out of the year. As early as age 10, Monroe was forced to skip school on many occasions so he could work the land, yet he still managed to flourish in his education.

When he was 16, Monroe was forced to drop out of school. His mother died in 1772, and his father passed away two years later, meaning James had to work to provide for his younger siblings. Soon after, his uncle took them in, and this was when James's life changed.

His uncle, Joseph Jones, was a member of the Virginia House of Burgesses, and he often took young James along with him to meetings. While there, James met people like Thomas Jefferson and George Washington, who would have a massive influence on him. Apart from this, his uncle also managed to score James a place in the College of William & Mary.

His time in college only lasted just over a year, as Monroe dropped out to help fight in the American Revolutionary War (1775–1783), which had just broken out. At 17, Monroe was made a lieutenant and was called north to fight in the New York and New Jersey campaign. In December, Monroe was part of the Battle of Trenton (discussed in the George Washington section). Although it was a success, he suffered a severed artery and nearly died.

Following his heroics, George Washington personally called out Monroe for his bravery and named him a captain.

When the war ended, Monroe returned home and began studying law under Thomas Jefferson. His reputation quickly grew, and he was soon elected to the Senate in 1790. His heroics in the war had not been forgotten, and he had learned a lot under Jefferson.

While in the Senate, one of his main jobs was trying to smooth things over with France. Tensions were still high between the two nations, and they were still at war. Although things would be tense for a long time yet, the connections Monroe made would help when signing the Louisiana Purchase a decade or so later.

Just before the turn of the century, James Monroe was named governor of Virginia. He continued in this role for three years and used it to create a better education system for the less fortunate people of America. He had seen how hard it could be for those without money to get a good education, and he knew that a well-educated America was a stronger one.

Monroe was soon thinking about the American

presidency, and after the Louisiana Purchase in 1803, he began making moves in that direction. During a visit back home to Virginia in 1807, Monroe was met by hordes of people singing his praises. They had heard stories about his heroics in the war and his major triumphs in politics, and they urged him to run for president in the next election. Their massive support convinced him, and he announced that he would run.

It wasn't until 1816 that Monroe made his move, though, and he won easily. He had been backed from the beginning by his good friend and 4th president, James Madison. Like Jefferson had done for Madison before, Madison did for Monroe, and his pleas to the public to vote for his friend worked.

Monroe went right to work, signing the Treaty of 1818, which stretched U.S. property from the Atlantic Ocean to the Pacific. A year later, he purchased Florida from the Spanish, growing America even more. His expansion of the nation started to make America one of the strongest powers in the world, and his next move cemented it.

After being easily reelected in 1820, he began work on the Monroe Doctrine. This policy set down ground rules for the rest of the world. It basically told them that America was the New World and that they would no longer get involved in conflicts outside of its borders, mainly in Europe. It also stated that any attempt at colonizing* a state in America by any other country would be seen as a hostile act and, therefore, a declaration of war.

James Monroe had set solid boundaries, and he declared that America would forever be its own nation. He had fought in the Revolutionary War, and he had no intention of giving up his or anyone else's freedom.

By the time Monroe stepped down in 1825, the states of Maine, Missouri, Alabama, Mississippi, and Illinois had become part of the Union. America had grown under his reign, and his time in office can be seen as very successful.

He retired to his home in Monroe Hill and spent much of his time at the University of Virginia, serving on the board alongside his good friends Thomas Jefferson and James Madison. After his wife died in 1830, Monroe moved to New York to live with his daughter but passed away less than a year later.

He died on July 4, 1831, making him the third president to have passed away on Independence Day. Quite unbelievably, three of the Founding Fathers—John Adams, Thomas Jefferson, and Monroe—all died on the anniversary of the Declaration of Independence. James Monroe may be one of the lesser-known presidents, but he is undoubtedly one of the most important.

WILLIAM MCKINLEY

SERVED AS PRESIDENT	AGE AT INAUGURATION	PRESIDENT NUMBER
1897-1901	54	25TH

PARTY	NICKNAME	HOMETOWN
REPUBLICAN	THE IDOL OF OHIO	NILES, OHIO

BIOGRAPHY

One of four American presidents to be assassinated, William McKinley is probably the least known of them. But his time in charge saw America have one of its greatest economic rises in history, and he was the man who signed the Treaty of Paris in 1898, effectively bringing a much-needed era of peace between the nations. He was a war hero who fought for his country for years and did it all while battling one of the fiercest enemies of all—depression.

William McKinley was born the seventh of nine children on January 29, 1843. He was initially raised in Niles, Ohio, but the family moved to Poland, Ohio when he was a boy as they searched for better schools for the children. They found them, and young William flourished in his more professional surroundings.

After graduating from Poland Seminary in 1859, he started at Allegheny College in Meadville, Pennsylvania. While there, he became an important member of the Sigma Alpha Epsilon fraternity and showed early signs of his leadership and organization.

But his time at Allegheny was cut short, and after just over a year, William returned home. He had fallen ill several times, which was since linked to the deep depression he had found himself in. William suffered from depression his whole life, and he did so at a time when mental health was completely ignored.

Thankfully today, we are much more aware of mental

health issues, and help is always available so that none of us have to fight it alone.

Once back in Ohio, McKinley began working as a postal clerk while also teaching at a local school on the side. This time of his life is recorded as being pretty standard, and it wasn't until the Civil War broke out in 1861 that his passion for his country truly took hold.

William McKinley had only turned 18 when he enrolled in the Union army as a private, and in just a month, he was sent into battle. His rank of private didn't last very long, and he was quickly promoted several times, becoming second lieutenant two years later.

McKinley fought on the front line until the war ended in 1865, then he moved back home again and began practicing law (of course he did!). His life seemed to find some regularity once more, but things changed in 1876 when he took on a massive public case representing local coal miners. They wanted more pay and better working conditions, and through McKinley's fantastic work in the courtroom, they were awarded them.

The victory shot McKinley into the public eye, and he became a local hero overnight. He was seen as a man of the people and someone who believed in helping the less fortunate to earn what they were worth. His newfound fame meant only one thing for him: a new adventure in politics.

Not even a year after the coal miners' court case, McKinley was a congressman. At first, he was given simple committee assignments, but he didn't take offense. Instead, he knuckled down and did whatever was asked of him to the best of his ability. McKinley could have pouted during this stage of his life, but his determination to work hard regardless of the conditions proved vitally important.

It was this attitude that finally brought him to the public's attention again. After years of loyal service in Congress, the people of Ohio literally begged him to run for governor. McKinley agreed, winning by a huge 20,000 vote margin. After that, the rest of his climb became a whole lot easier.

When exactly William McKinley made the decision to run for president is a little unclear. He kept no diaries or documents regarding this period, and no letters have survived. It is suspected that around 1888—eight years before the 1896 election—McKinley and a wealthy businessman named Mark Hanna began making plans to run someday in the future.

Hanna was a loyal supporter of McKinley and believed in his policies wholeheartedly. He spent the equivalent of millions over the next decade helping to promote William McKinley for president.

After many years of campaigning, McKinley was sworn in on March 4, 1897. He told the people right away that he would fix the currency issue, which had divided opinion for far too long, and that America would cease going to war for anything other than protecting their own lands. This meant that America would no longer look to take land from other countries.

A year after his inauguration, Spanish forces attacked American soldiers in Cuba, and McKinley was left with no option but to declare war. As he had promised, America only fought because they had been forced to react. What started as a small battle in Cuba became the Spanish-American War (1898), and it continued for another 100 days.

But his time in office wasn't all conflict. Later that same year, McKinley signed the Treaty of Paris, finally bringing peace with France. Along with the improving economy, the treaty made McKinley even more popular. He had stuck to the promises he'd made when running for president, and the people respected him for that. Too many presidents lie during their campaigns to win votes, then never follow through with everything they swore they would do once in power.

When the next election came along, McKinley was voted back in easily. He had won the public's trust, and those in his Senate felt the same way. Unfortunately, his second term didn't last very long, and a tragic event took away a president who was in the prime of his life and currently flourishing in office.

Less than a year into his second term, William McKinley was shot twice in the stomach at close range by an anarchist* named Leon Czolgosz. As everyone at the scene began to panic, McKinley—who was losing a lot of blood—remained in charge. Even as he was slipping away, he calmly told those around him to break the news gently to his wife, Ida. When the angry crowd got a hold of the gunman and prepared to lynch* him, McKinley asked them to stop, essentially saving Czolgosz's life.

Amazingly, he survived for a week following the shooting. But it wasn't to be, and when he took a bad turn on the seventh day, the doctors knew his time had come. They discovered after his death that gangrene had set in on the walls of his stomach, and it had been slowly poisoning his blood.

McKinley passed away on September 14, 1901, at the age of 58. His vice president, Theodore Roosevelt, rushed back to Buffalo to be sworn in as the 26th president of America, and a new age began.

William McKinley will be forever remembered as a man of honor who strove for peace. He was a man who fought for his country alongside George Washington and left the army a national hero. He was humble and fair, which was never more evident when he demanded mercy for the man who had just shot him.

GLOSSARY

Allies - A group of nations—mainly America, Britain, and Japan—who came together to stop Nazi Germany, Italy, and Japan during World War II.

Anarchist - Someone who tries to overthrow people in power, usually through violence or protests.

Attorney - A lawyer.

Bay of Pigs - A curved bay in southern Cuba where America failed during an invasion.

Boys Nation - A group that chooses 100 exceptional students for further education in things like leadership and civics.

Cabinet - A group of government officials—usually led by the vice president—who debate new laws, etc., before presenting them to the president.

Colonizing - When one nation or group takes over another nation, city, or place and makes it its own.

Continental Army - It was the army of the United Colonies, representing the thirteen colonies that later became the United States.

Corruption - Cheating and stealing by those in power, usually by way of bribes.

Cuban Missile Crisis - A panicked October in 1962 when the world came as close as it ever had been to nuclear war. The tensions were between America and the USSR (Russia).

Dictatorship - A dictator is someone who rules a country with total power, usually with violence and oppression.

Electors - These can be the common people who vote but are usually those in government voting for their own people's promotions.

Founding Fathers - A group of people who founded a nation. In America's case, they are considered to be John Adams, Benjamin Franklin, Alexander Hamilton, John Jay, Thomas Jefferson, James Madison, and George Washington.

Great Depression - A time of severe poverty across America that started with the Wall Street Crash in 1929 and didn't fully end until 1940.

Guerilla Tactics - A way for smaller groups to attack and beat larger ones, usually by way of ambush.

House of Burgesses - An early meeting of government officials that began in Virginia.

Ivy League - A group of eight selected education institutions consisting of colleges, such as Harvard and Princeton, that are generally considered to be the best and most expensive colleges in the country.

Legislation - The creation of laws, usually by a group or committee.

Lynch - When a group of people kills another without a trial.

Militia - An army formed by civilians, sometimes to assist the real army or often to rise up against a government.

NATO - North Atlantic Treaty Organization. A group of 30 nations—28 in Europe plus the USA and Canada— that meet regularly to discuss world matters and keep the peace.

Pass the bar - Officially called the Uniform Bar Examination (UBE), and often shortened to "the bar." To "pass the bar" is to pass the exam that allows one to become a lawyer.

Polio - A disease that can cause paralysis and sometimes death. It spread through America in the early 1950s, causing much suffering and fear.

Recession - A period in time when the economy suffers badly. It usually causes mass unemployment and sometimes poverty.

Russo-Japanese War - A short-fought war between Russia and Japan.

Segregation - The forced separation of people, usually because of skin color or religious beliefs.

Senate - A group of people just under the president selected by voters to decide on laws, etc.

Smear campaign - A plan to destroy the character of a political opponent, usually through lies in newspapers and other media.

Wall Street Crash - A stock market crash in 1929 that nearly crippled America financially. It was the worst of its kind in history.

Western - Also referred to as the "Western World," it is usually considered to be nations such as America, Canada, and Europe.

Women's suffrage - A movement that tried to get women more rights, mainly the right to vote.

Printed in Great Britain
by Amazon

39480832R00066